PRAISE FOR *WILD NIGHTS OUT*

'So inspiring! Reading *Wild Nights Out* is like being given an invitation to a whole new dimension of life. Exploring and nature spotting don't need to stop when the sun goes down. For grown-ups, children, and anyone in between, this book offers guidance, ideas, challenges to try and games to play in the dusk and dark. But, more than anything else, it encourages us to cross a threshold into a new world and go on a nocturnal ramble to look and listen for where the wild things are.'

Simon Reeve, author and broadcaster

'If you are a creature intrigued about the dimpsy hours and its goings-on, this is the perfect companion for your adventures. As the planet spins us away from the sun, a world less explored is to be found – a time of new creatures, celestial bodies, new sights, sounds and smells. This book gently holds your hand and guides you into the mysterious folds of the darkness, helping you get the most out of the night. Nocturnal empowerment for the curious.'

Nick Baker, naturalist, TV presenter and author

'If you once wished the days to never end, with Chris's glorious and concise re-enchantment of the night, you too will soon become a nocturnal convert, willing your children to stay up and out as late as possible. *Wild Nights Out* isn't so much about conquering the fear of the dark but redeeming this realm through ancient and intrepid means of befriending it, inspiring wonderful ways to play beyond the reach of electricity's falsifying security.'

Sam Lee, folk singer, Radio 4 presenter, and Mercury Prize–nominated artist

'Chris Salisbury knows of what he speaks. This storyteller has been thoroughly drubbed in nature's mood swings and come up the wiser for it. *Wild Nights Out* is an inventive mapping of that accumulated knowledge. Long before it was even vaguely fashionable, Chris was walking the roads of wildness and story, and this book is a lovely testament to his devotion. Both pragmatic and poetic, *Wild Nights Out* will be a worthy companion for anyone who yearns for a fresh and unexpected relationship to the living world. There are big, powerful energies out there in the dark, and a few have slipped into this book, chewing on its edges.'

Dr Martin Shaw, author of *Smoke Hole* and *Courting the Wild Twin*

'A fantastic mix of usefulness and imagination, of practical experience and love for the living world.'

Jay Griffiths, author of *Kith* and *Wild: An Elemental Journey*

'*Wild Nights Out* is the night's song, seducing us like a siren on a rock, beckoning us to dive deep into an enchanted world. Chris Salisbury has collated a hundred reasons to step over this threshold and explore, perhaps for the first time, the wonder of the wild night. Stars, stories, songs and games come out of his wizard's hat to reacquaint us with the mysteries of nocturnal nature. As an educator and parent, I'm so glad this book has been offered to a world hungry for meaning and connection.'

Charlotte Church, singer and broadcaster;
founder, Awen Project

'In his wonderful book, *Wild Nights Out,* Chris Salisbury reminds us of so many things forgotten. The night is truly fully half of our lives. Yet today we live as if we only experience the day. Through his wonderful stories, lore, science and accessible activities, Chris helps us remember that we are, as humans, at least half darkness. Through the journey of *Wild Nights Out*, we are remembering the part of us that has been hidden in recent times, and it's like meeting a long-lost relative that we truly love.'

Jon Young, author of *Coyote's Guide to Connecting with Nature* and *What the Robin Knows*

'*Wild Nights Out* is a masterful guide for night walks. Chock-full of engaging games and fascinating information, this book makes leading night-time excursions a joy. Chris Salisbury has created a magnificent and comprehensive resource for anyone who loves the night.'

Joseph Bharat Cornell, author of *Sharing Nature*,
Deep Nature Play, and *Flow Learning*

'Chris Salisbury is a consummate guide to the night and its chrysalis-like capacity to convert us from sailors of safe harbors to celebrants of uncharted seas – wanderers amidst nocturnal creatures (like owls, bats, and badgers) or the existential conundrums that the night sky elicits (like *Why are we here?*). Chris doesn't resolve the frights and riddles of the dark, but deftly draws us in, supporting us to make our own dazzling discoveries and to be shape-shifted by our night-walk odysseys. *Wild Nights Out*: don't go into the dark without it.'

Bill Plotkin, PhD, author of *Soulcraft* and *The Journey of Soul Initiation*

'*Wild Nights Out* is neatly book ended with the question *why is it dark?* and takes the practitioner on a journey exploring this and many other questions about the shady side of the planet. It is not just Chris's inimitable poetry that make this such a great read, it is the enticing experiences and journeys into the night that Chris takes us on that we can easily replicate, adapt and conduct with our groups of learners which will help relate to and answer those questions of the night. This book is packed full of activities for immersing learners in the world of dusk to dawn that can be adapted for any age and gives the all-important health and safety tips to help people feel comfortable and yet still feel the nervous anticipation, excitement and beauty of the darkened hours. There are poems and stories, ways to use stories around the campfire, lots of natural history and 'tuning in' activities and titbits, journeys into different habitats – from the river to the seashore, and of course ways of magically interacting with the night sky.'

Jon Cree, founding chair, Forest School Association;
coauthor of *The Essential Guide to Forest School and Nature Pedagogy*;
veteran educator and nature connection trainer

'Chris Salisbury is without doubt one of the world's foremost outdoor ecological educators. In this marvellously well-written book, Chris shares his decades of wisdom and experience about how to bring children into the presence of the night as a living being, with her sounds, sights, smells, depths and imaginings. Even if you don't use this book with children specifically in mind, like me, you'll be enchanted from start to finish by its capacity to introduce you and people of all ages to the wonders of the night. You'll feel a powerful urge to go out into the night yourself with Chris and his book as guides to wake up your forgotten child's vivid perceptions of nature.'

Dr Stephan Harding, Deep Ecology Research Fellow,
senior lecturer in Holistic Science, Schumacher College, Dartington, UK

'Chris Salisbury piques curiosity in such a way that brings people beyond knowledge and information, and into meaningful and real connection and relationship. As a storyteller and educator, his ability to weave together natural history, science, story, poetry, and myth in a graceful and compelling way is evident among these pages. I see it as critical to provide educators, and people in general, not just with good information, natural history, and science, but also with brilliant strategies for bringing people along for the ride in a way that is fun, creative, and artistic. Advocates for the human right to deeply connect to place could well use a guide that helps us find narratives that weave together in a soulful approach to the lifelong journey of falling in love with the earth. *Wild Nights Out* helps us do that.'

Marcus Reynerson, adult immersion program manager
and lead instructor, Wilderness Awareness School

'I cannot think of a better all-round book to enchant your family's evening walk or an enthralling night-time adventure with groups of children or adults. It offers a wealth of nature-connecting ideas, stories and games. All convey Chris Salisbury's deep involvement with the creation of fabulous darkness experiences in the outdoors. The book belongs in every family home and library. Buy it.'

Dr Alida Gersie, author of *Earthtales* and *Storytelling for a Greener World*

'Like the storyteller he is, Chris leads us by enchantment into the beauty and depth of the dark. He entices us into its warm embrace – to remember, to listen, to feel part of something unseen once again. His book is rich in poetry and fact, as practical as it is, a conjuring of our interest in something so hidden, we may have forgotten it ever existed. He takes us by the hand and leaves traces for us to follow – each in our own way, an adventure that calls every time we close our eyes.'

Ya'Acov Darling Khan, author of *Jaguar in the Body, Butterfly in the Heart* and *Shaman: Invoking Power, Presence and Purpose at the Core of Who You Are*

'This book is an invitation to step out of the everyday world and into the darkness, and to find the night wonderful: wild and rich and beautiful. Chris takes us on a journey through landscapes and starscapes and species, experiencing the nocturnal world through all our senses. He offers ways to absorb, understand and use those experiences to leave us inspired, finding new strength and joy to change how we live in this world for the better.'

Gordon MacLellan, author and environmental trainer

'A delightful, mysterious, compelling work born of Chris Salisbury's lifetime love of nature. This wonderful book is like the night itself, daring us to step outside and, wrapped in shadows, become alive to that we can only ever fleetingly behold.'

Mac Macartney, author, speaker, change-maker

'*Wild Nights Out* is an intoxicating cocktail of outdoor activities and inspirations, and one that every environmental educator has been longing for, even if he or she hadn't realised that before reading it. Here is the realm of night, unwrapped for us by Salisbury like rich jewels on black velvet. Informative, resourceful, packed with wisdom and wit, this is a book for all ages and all times – a book that connects us with the wild natural world that awaits, as raw and relevant today as it was to our ancestors generations ago.'

Prof Clayton MacKenzie, provost and interim president, Hong Kong Baptist University

WILD NIGHTS OUT

The Magic of Exploring the Outdoors after Dark

CHRIS SALISBURY

Chelsea Green Publishing
White River Junction, Vermont
London, UK

Commissioning Editor: Jonathan Rae
Developmental Editor: Fern Marshall Bradley
Copy Editor: Susan Pegg
Proofreader: Nikki Sinclair
Indexer: Lisa Himes
Designer: Melissa Jacobson
Page Layout: Abrah Griggs

Printed in Canada.
First printing May 2021.
10 9 8 7 6 5 4 3 2 1   21 22 23 24 25

Our Commitment to Green Publishing
Chelsea Green sees publishing as a tool for cultural change and ecological stewardship. We strive to align our book manufacturing practices with our editorial mission and to reduce the impact of our business enterprise in the environment. We print our books and catalogs on chlorine-free recycled paper, using vegetable-based inks whenever possible. This book may cost slightly more because it was printed on paper that contains recycled fiber, and we hope you'll agree that it's worth it. *Wild Nights Out* was printed on paper supplied by Marquis that is made of recycled materials and other controlled sources.

Library of Congress Cataloging-in-Publication Data
Names: Salisbury, Chris, 1965- author.
Title: Wild nights out : the magic of exploring the outdoors after dark / Chris Salisbury.
Description: White River Junction, Vermont : Chelsea Green Publishing, 2021. | Includes bibliographical references and index.
Identifiers: LCCN 2021005649 (print) | LCCN 2021005650 (ebook) | ISBN 9781603589932 (paperback) | ISBN 9781603589949 (ebook)
Subjects: LCSH: Outdoor life — Miscellanea. | Night — Miscellanea. | Nocturnal animals — Miscellanea. | Constellations — Miscellanea.
Classification: LCC GV191.6 .S25 2021 (print) | LCC GV191.6 (ebook) | DDC 796.5 — dc23
LC record available at https://lccn.loc.gov/2021005649
LC ebook record available at https://lccn.loc.gov/2021005650

Chelsea Green Publishing
85 North Main Street, Suite 120
White River Junction, Vermont USA

Somerset House
London, UK

www.chelseagreen.com

The deepest gratitude is for my beloved wife, Reeba, for all her faith, support and wild intelligence. Most of all, this book is dedicated to the seven generations that follow us. May your excursions into the night be filled with enchantment and wonder.

CONTENTS

FOREWORD

I spent a lot of my late teens and early twenties in the dark. I studied badgers and I very quickly learned that artificial light was my enemy. I still regularly explore the woods at night – but never with a torch. It takes me about forty-five minutes to establish my night vision and just a second with a torch to lose it. Then I 'blind' myself, and everything else can see where I am – not good! And, besides, where I walk is sadly never dark – the glimmer of the city always haunts my skies.

Obviously, as a naturalist, I want to overcome the perceived inaccessibility of the night, to meet and study nocturnal animals, to dispel the myths that inhabit their reputations and revel in their fabulous behaviours. But being comfortable, alone in the woods in the dark, offers me so much more.

A fear of fear is a tragic contemporary trope. When was the last time you were really frightened? When you felt that sizzling surge of life, that balloon inflate in the pit of your stomach and the dizzying stab of panic bouncing around your brain? Fear does have a smell. Do you know it? Sadly, I doubt it. … We are swaddled in comfort, protected from perhaps our most primal and essential emotion, denied the full breadth of our life experience. Such experience is fed by our senses and, as a diurnal animal, with our sight being pre-eminent, darkness – effectively 'blindness' – is a daily source of fear. The mass availability and access to artificial light has bleached that beautiful blackness for visual clarity. We've wounded but not killed the night. This book is a wonderful invitation to rediscover the dark and all the things that cry, creep or glow there. In a world clamouring for inclusivity, the banishment of light to reveal another world is very welcome indeed.

The solitary peace, the true comfort of isolation, the simplicity of the ancient experience, the sense of freedom fed by the small bravery of eschewing the need for light, the self-control and sense of empowerment – all these fuse with the eerie wails of foxes, the screams of owls, the quiet conversations of mice, the twinkle of the stars and the smiling saucer of the moon to offer a real and revelatory therapy. Being out in the night is invigorating and uplifting and, if you accept the offer that Salisbury has cleverly crafted here and gently ease yourself and your children into the darkness, it will undoubtedly light up your life.

CHRIS PACKHAM
New Forest 2021

DUSK

The beginning of anything is always a 'threshold' moment. The word derives from olden times and referred to the dedicated space at the edge of the village where the grain was threshed. As such, it represents the zone between the village and the wild world, between what is known and what holds mystery. It befits a book about the dark that we pause and dwell briefly in the liminal space between the day and the night to make conscious our stepping over of a threshold. This positions us, and the book, appropriately to be fully present to the gifts the night-time will bring, if we are fully attentive to the experience. This place we have many names for: dusk, gloaming, cockshut, grosping, crow-time, owl-leet and dimpsy.

No other phase of the day or night has inspired more terminology in the English language than the twilight zone and the bit that follows it i.e. dusk, the betwixt and between of the story world. When night traditionally ushered in the fear and trepidation of known and unknown threats, it's not surprising that it dominated our attention, and imagination, with so many expressive idioms. Irish Gaelic, for example, has four terms just to chart the successive phases from late afternoon to nightfall.

In Britain we can anticipate a rich array of wildlife at this time, like being at a junction or crossroads with plenty of 'traffic' abroad, either returning to burrow or nest to take refuge from the night-time threats, or emerging to take advantage of what the night has to offer. On this threshold, our consciousness can relax into the tranquillity that often accompanies the twilight, and simultaneously our awareness heightens, attuned to what might be lurking in the twilight. It's this special moment, like that brief period when the tide turns, when an influx of new possibilities combines with the outbreath of the day ending. As Antoine de Saint-Exupery says in *Flight to Arras*, its 'when words fade and things come alive. When the destructive analysis of day is done.' It's a time therefore that is ripe for sitting in reflection and contemplation of the day that has gone, as well as a moment for attunement to what is to come…

Introduction

*Everything has its wonders, even darkness and silence, and I learn,
whatever state I may be in, therein to be content.*

HELEN KELLER

W ho's afraid of the dark?

'Sssshhhhh. … Did you hear that?' Worried looks spread like soft butter on bread on the faces of twenty mildly panicked primary schoolchildren who shuffle clumsily closer to me, their nightwalk leader. 'That was a tawny owl hooting – shall we go and try to see it?' I ask them.

'Yes, yes, yes!' whisper-shout the children, who can hardly contain their fear and excitement at the prospect of going into the woods at night without using their torches. 'Let's try to use our night vision,' I had told them, 'at least for the first part of the trail. It's surprising how much you can see in the dark when your eyes have not been exposed to artificial light.'

After the role-play of pulling down a 'veil of silence' over our heads, we head off in muffled excitement, like a huddle of young partridges, into the trees. A small hand creeps into mine for reassurance – Jessica has never been without a light at night, let alone into the fairy-tale domain of the woods in the dark. After their initial bravado around the bright campfire, all the children are humbled into a respectful silence by this threshold moment in their lives, their first nocturnal ramble in the dark to look and listen for where the wild things are.

'I can't see!' whimpers William, and I slow the pace to let his expectations catch up with his actual experience, until we arrive in a small clearing under the generous spread of beech boughs.

'Well done,' I say. 'You navigated the path by starlight and moonlight, just like some of the nocturnal animals that we've come to find. Now, hold still, and listen,' I whisper, and our forty-two animal ears reach out into the mysterious stillness.

Soon Harriet whispers back, 'I can't hear anything.'

'Exactly!' I respond. 'Did you ever *hear nothing* before?' (Cue the silent shaking of heads.) 'Well, boys and girls, that is the sound of silence: the sound of nothing at all. … Until some night-time creature enters the silent stage. Now, what sort of noises might we expect to hear on our woodland nightwalk?'

Teaching the curious, as every parent and educator knows, is wholly different from teaching the indifferent. The outdoor environment, particularly a diverse nature reserve, will always stimulate the visitor, unless, of course, bad weather intervenes.

Unlike the familiarity of the everyday home and classroom environment, a natural setting will prompt a different set of responses from children that is not entirely predictable. Children we think we know very well will reveal themselves in unexpected ways as they react to new stimuli. It's a good reminder not to make too many assumptions about our learners.

Under the cover of darkness, our familiar environments are transformed into something mysterious. The terrain we know so well by day takes on another character by night, and our indifference can instantly be forgotten when we find ourselves exploring it. Even your own living room at home becomes another kind of adventure playground in the dark. Of course, we reach for the electric light switch instinctively, to banish the night, without a second thought. But those of us who played in the darkness as children, even in the comfort of our own homes, were charged up with an intense feeling of excitement and adventure. I can remember a thousand 'night missions' navigating through my house as a boy, with the lights turned out, mostly on my way to my bedroom. When I was younger, the short little route to my bedroom was fraught with 'danger' in the form of menacing nocturnal beings I imagined lurking in the shadows, even when the lights were on. After being sent to bed, I would linger as long as I could, entertaining myself in front of the hallway mirror until I heard the sound of my parents coming, whereupon I would scurry up the stairs for fear of being caught. For many years of my childhood, I read books in bed at night in an attempt to put off the inevitable moment when I had to turn out the light, again when I heard Mum or Dad climbing the stairs.

So, as you read this book, remember to pause and imagine what it's like to be a child in an unfamiliar place, like a forest, under the enchantment of the night-time…

Very exciting indeed.

About This Book

This book is designed to be an aid to parents, grandparents, teachers and those wonderful ambassadors of nature, the outdoor professionals who introduce young people to the natural world. There has been a paucity of material to support excursions into the night-time, and I offer *Wild Nights Out* as a helpful handbook of ideas, information and activities distilled from twenty-five years' experience leading groups into nocturnal nature on events ranging from nightwalks and overnight wildlife experiences to week-long camps with schoolchildren and excluded teenagers, as well as community, corporate and family groups.

I hope to bridge a gap by writing about the dark from both a practical perspective and a cultural one. We impoverish ourselves in avoiding the darkness in the way that we do, brightening our world with the constant hum of electric light. As I discuss in the opening chapter, the somewhat forgotten dimension of nature at night offers so much, it seems a shame not to take advantage of the potential enrichment that can be obtained by doing a few things in the dark.

Before you plunge headlong into a dark thicket, however, some investment in preparation is going to be worthwhile. In chapter 2, I focus on the senses, as this heightened awareness of our innate capacities will enable a deeper engagement with the night-time. This information will also add texture to the accompanying narratives in your role as guide. If they get a bit too technical, by all means move on to the elements that attract your interest. You can always refer back once your curiosity is aroused by some night-time immersions.

I also introduce some technical equipment options, which may or may not be of interest, depending on your nocturnal needs. The principle remains the same: to harness the potential of some night-time aids to take us further into the connection we seek with the dark.

Chapter 3 is the first of several filled with activities. I begin with suggestions on how to make use of the twilight hours for some attunement, as this time of day offers ideal preparation and educational opportunity before stepping over the threshold and heading into the night. From there, the activities expand to a wide and diverse range of 'things to do' in the dark, which can be mixed and matched accordingly.

I have included some natural history throughout the book, which, although by no means exhaustive, will help you develop some affinity for nocturnal creatures and the night sky, and add texture to stories that you tell before or after an activity or as part of a nightwalk. The aim, after all, is for everyone to become more interested in wildlife, and a little storytelling goes a long way to help broker that connection.

There is so much to fascinate and intrigue for the naturalist, given privileged access to specific species at night, and there is some information in chapter 4 about nocturnal nature in Britain to help focus teachers, educators and parents on the wildlife side of things.

Chapter 5 introduces stargazing, and I offer activities, some scientific experimentation and star lore to support the general fascination with the great mystery of the night sky. It's limited in scope, because it's such a vast subject, but I hope there is enough to garner your interest and further your relationship to the stars.

Facilitation skills are a distinct advantage for leading the activities in this book, and will come with experience. If you are planning a full programme, the activity mix you decide upon is not necessarily critical, but I include several suggested sequences for a nightwalk in chapter 6 that you can follow as described or use as inspiration for curating the right blend for the occasion. Common sense will guide you to a programme commensurate with the general chronology of the arriving and deepening dark, and meeting the creatures contained therein.

In chapter 7, Campfire Time, I focus on creating enjoyable experiences around the fire – such a wonderful ingredient of a night-time event for those that have the good fortune to experience it. I hope the ideas and material I share for holding space for a group inspire some quality times around a fireside.

Finally, this is a book written within the context of northern Europe, and in particular from my love affair with Britain. If you are reading this from outside this geographical area, there are some parts that obviously will not pertain to your bioregion. That said, most of it can still apply and, with some adaptations, remain a banquet of resources and inspiration for night-time wanderings, wherever you are.

CHAPTER 1

Introducing the Dark

How insupportable would be the days,
if the night with its dews and darkness did not
come to restore the drooping world.
HENRY DAVID THOREAU, *Night and Moonlight*

I
n 1880, Joseph Swan's home in North East England was the first to be fitted with his newly invented incandescent electric lighting, enabling continuous bright light and heralding a new dawn for humanity. Although it sounds grandiose, it could be said that our world has been profoundly altered ever since.

In so many ways the opportunity for continuous light was a boon for humanity, its advantages obvious to all. What is rarely considered, however, is the loss of something very precious. On that night, in the compulsively expanding growth-culture of the newly industrialised human world, the darkness was symbolically banished and we became exiled from its mystery, enchantment and psychic grasp. It's not that you can't find darkness at all anymore, but it is now located somewhere other than where most people live. The National Geographic quote a 2016 study estimating that ninety-nine per cent of Europe and America are affected by light pollution.

Our obsession with brightening our environment ensures that even the dusk is lit by streetlights that burn through till dawn. There is no string to pull or switch to flick if you want a few hours off to bathe in the quiet enveloping dark. You have to go out of town to find that sanctuary.

There are accusations of profligacy to level at this industrial all-night brightening of the dark. According to the International Dark Sky

Association, 'at least 30 per cent of all outdoor lighting in the U.S. alone is wasted, adding up to $3.3 billion and the release of 21 million tons of carbon dioxide per year! To offset all that carbon dioxide, we'd have to plant 875 million trees annually.'

However, this is not a rant against light per se. The advent of fire and then subtle forms of illumination like the first oil lamps ten thousand years ago brought shadows and shapes, softening the dark into something less foreboding and more enchanting. The high contrast of artificial bright lights, however, compromises our physical senses and makes the darkness more impenetrable and uninviting. To lose all ability to see is disorientating, and frightening for a sight-dominated species. We have a biological, in-built fear of what we cannot see, which is emphasised more when we have no intimacy with a place. As the old proverb from the Zuni people in North America goes, 'After dark, all cats are leopards.' It's natural to feel scared of the dark, and I don't even mean pitch-black conditions, which are rare to experience in the outdoors, but rather the natural dark regulated by moon and starlight. I know many adults who retain their childhood fear and reach quickly for the light switch when confronted by darkness.

Redeeming the Dark

As my three daughters were growing up, I observed in them the transition from the sweet innocence of their early years when they seemed unafraid of the dark and similarly unafraid of the forest that surrounded our cottage. Something happened to change their perception and it seemed they had quite suddenly learnt to fear any environment where they could not see clearly. I was curious as to why, because I had not consciously taught them fear, or told them of unseen dangers. Indeed, they were oblivious to any tangible threat from beast or bandit.

I continue to ponder whether fear of darkness is biological or cultural. For example, do children pick up fear of the dark through the fairy tales they are told from an early age, or from adult behaviour that models a fear of the dark? Or is it simply a biological requirement, a necessary kind of survival strategy from times past when the danger from animal attack was present and real? As they used to say in Tuscany, 'Whoever goes out at night, looks for death.'

Whether the source of the fear is biological or cultural, my own perception is that it is more pronounced in our contemporary culture that has exiled itself from living close to, and intimately with, the land and its natural cloak of darkness.

There is a cultural symbolism, too, in turning on bright lights. The further we get from living with natural rhythms, the more uncomfortable we seem to be with natural darkness. In our language, we have relegated the concepts of darkness and night-time to the negative, as reflected in expressions like having 'dark thoughts' or 'nightmares', 'the dark side' and 'casting a dark shadow'.

If our tendency to tame the darkness has its roots in our primitive survival mechanism, something seems to have changed in terms of our cultural perception of the dark. I propose that the *soulful* quality of the night-time has been lost, as we have strayed far from the path of living a dynamic, reciprocal exchange with nature that offered our predecessors so much texture and meaning within the rhythm of light and dark.

In the old rhythm, dusk was the transition between what went before and the deepening gloom and drop in temperature that necessitated kindling the fire and gathering around it. In that old, simple way, the community would reconstitute itself and process the day. Lamplight and firelight would meet with the dark and resolve into shadows, with long fingers of soft light and black night interplaying in movement that replicated an animate, dynamic, mysterious world. Nothing to be 'done' by night. (That said, in the pre-industrial era, and across the world, it was the common habit to have 'two sleeps' during the night, interrupted by a brief passage of time in the middle, for all sorts of nocturnal activity. Our assumption of the need for a continuous night of sleep, it appears, is a more modern phenomenon.

In brightening the dark, we extend the day, and our activity can continue unabated. The bright, constant artificial lights of the contemporary night scene leave nothing to the imagination – they imitate daylight rather than soft night light. We simply continue to go about our business as usual, no matter the hour.

As mythologist Martin Shaw writes in *Scatterlings*, 'Night always carries its liminal invitation.' It's like the stories we love to hear, adults as well as children; unlike theatre or film, which offer the complete picture for our eyes and ears to enjoy, the spoken narrative offers only words for our ears. But our imagination is activated by what our eyes cannot clearly see, conjuring up pictures that form instantly within our own internal cinema. In the same way, by allowing the dark to be a presence in our waking lives, the 'not seeing' stimulates our imagination and dreaming. Many traditional tales include the character of a blind person who dispenses wisdom – as if there is a 'deeper sight' that is gifted from total darkness. In Norse myth, the god Odin who removed his own eye became 'one-eyed but twice sighted'.

Subtle changes can take place at night in the ways we interact with one another. As we feel more exposed by the imagined, or real, threat that the night poses, we are brought close together by an implicit understanding of our vulnerability, which is part of our common humanity. In the soft shadows of firelight or lamplight, we subconsciously remember the continuum in which humans have gathered around the hearth, the place of safety and community, for thousands of years. This is especially emphasised on camp, when we circle up around the fire and the night looms large all around us, perhaps magnified by the bright flames and shimmering sparks. As well as the sense of wonder, there is an unspoken communion that binds us together in the deep, and humbling mystery of the dark.

It strikes me as culturally significant that at the winter solstice, we now celebrate with a commercial bonanza. This is the darkest time of the year in the northern hemisphere, when all of the natural signs and rhythms suggest a reflective, introspective season. Yet we keep our ourselves diverted and distracted from the deepening dark with the bright, flashing lights and gaudy decorations of Christmas. It's not that our pagan ancestors didn't hold celebrations during the dark times of the year. There were sacramental feasts, for example, that would take place during the first full moon after the winter solstice, a ritual of gratitude for the returning light. I have nothing against celebrations, and certainly not the opportunity for family gatherings and old traditions, but the way it now plays out seems to pile commercial pressure and stress on many families. But perhaps we defer to this diversion so readily because it's preferable to a long winter enveloped in the soft, slow, penetrative dark.

Walking with a friend in the dark is better than walking alone in the light.   HELEN KELLER

Plants demonstrate so clearly the natural response to the dark and cold onset of autumn and winter, drawing down deep into their rooty essence, into the soil, conserving resources, until the conditions for growth and activity return. Some of our fellow mammals adapt to the dark and cold of winter by retreating into hibernation, riding the seasonal tides to make the most of food supplies and conserving energy. Of course, with the shops full all year round, and the advent of central heating and electric light, this kind of seasonal shift is no longer necessary for human folk.

There is profit in the dark for those who attune to its renewing, restful qualities. Think of it like a good night's sleep, and how much better we feel for it, ready to face the day. A raft of evidence has surfaced through extensive research showing fundamental health benefits from exposure to the dark, which I discuss later in this chapter. Complementing this, the night offers us sweet sanctuary from to-do lists and deadlines, from clock-watching and schedules, from having to be someone or something. Thus, I encourage you to consciously step over that threshold – let your eyes and circadian rhythms acclimatise, and set off on a moonlit trail that leads somewhere mysterious and enchanting. Nocturnal nature also awaits, in all its miraculous diversity and 'otherness', and whatever your location, it can never fail to interest, whether you are out on a solitary ramble or leading a group of excited children on a forest nightwalk.

The Bible proclaims, '"Let there be light," and there was light.' May I suggest we need to remember to turn the light *off* sometimes, too...

Defining the Dark

From one North American indigenous perspective, the dark is defined as an 'absence of light'. And whilst that is commensurate with our own succinct attempts to define it, the contemporary scientific version suggests that astronomical dusk arrives after sunset when the sun is 18 degrees below the horizon. Even then, because so much light pollution prevails, you might have to venture out into a desert or an open sea to experience it properly. Further to this, just because we can't see it doesn't mean light isn't present. Nanoscience helps us to determine that photons of light are present even in conditions that humans experience as 'pitch-black' night. However, I suggest that what is really relevant for us as experiential, sensory beings is the 'perception of the dark': when the night seems as black as coal, then, effectively, for our experience, it is. Fair enough?

But, we still need to ask the proverbial million-dollar question. The one that will puzzle, challenge and infuriate until the sweet elixir of understanding arrives. It's the ultimate riddle, as simple as it is confounding, but one that deserves to be in a book about the dark.

Why is it dark?

The answer seems obvious at first: it's because the great lantern in the sky has slipped below the horizon, right?

Wrong.

So then, why is it dark at night?

This clearly requires some more thought, or more dreaming.

I'm going to leave you to stew on this for a while and enjoy dwelling in the richness of the enquiry. Also, I want to observe the protocol of a proper riddle, which is not to simply give the answer away. You will find the answer as you read your way to the end of this book. Then you'll be ready to ask your companions this question, too, as you lead them out on a nightwalk.

Dark Medicine

As I hinted above, it turns out the dark is good for you – or rather, exposure to it has a positive implication for well-being.

That said, we are hardwired, biologically speaking, to retreat from the darkness because of the threats, real or imagined, that potentially lurk there. In fact, to give it the correct term, those that take this one stage further are achluophobic, meaning they have a deep fear of darkness.

In general, living creatures need periods of activity and rest, and the interchange between light and dark help our circadian rhythms.

However, there is now a proliferation of artificial light; 60 per cent of Europeans and 80 per cent of North Americans are living where they can't behold the Milky Way in the night sky because of light pollution.

This significant shift away from our long history of living half our lives in darkness must be having an impact. Research is now evidencing that a deprivation of darkness is indeed taking its toll on our rhythms, moods and well-being. Richard Stevens an epidemiologist at the University of

Connecticut, after decades of study into the effects of this deprivation on our health is unequivocal in his summary: 'What we need is a longer period of physiological nighttime.'

And that's just from a human perspective – we know that the effect of constant artificial light through the night is also detrimental to many other species.

When we understand some basic biology, it's easier to make the case for darkness as a sort of natural medicine. The gist of it is that when certain specialised neuron cells in the eye register declining light levels, a message is sent to the pineal gland in the brain, which then starts to release melatonin into the bloodstream. Melatonin is a hormone produced by your body and helps control your sleep. This 'darkness hormone', amongst other effects, dilates the blood vessels so the body temperature cools, which has the effect of making the body feel tired. It's also an important antioxidant to protect cells from harm, as well as a stimulant for our immune system to activate white blood cells at night.

There are certain cells in the retina that send a message to the brain to reduce the amount of melatonin released when exposed to the blue light present in contemporary lighting systems like LEDs. Blue light triggers our 'fight or flight' response – and so it's clear to see how the use of blue light in streetlamps, and especially to illuminate screens on electronic devices, is affecting sleep patterns. While we sleep, our bodies work to restore and replenish themselves, and these tasks are compromised when artificial lighting interferes with restful sleep.

So in 'light' of all this research and common sense, the general conclusion is that the dark is good for you, and there are simple steps to adjust your home environment to invite the darkness back into your night-time rest. The sleep clinics and sleep doctors are now contributing to well-being protocols and have much advice to give in this respect. For example, limit LED screen time and put up light-excluding blinds or curtains for the windows in the rooms you commonly use after dark.

The most interesting way to immerse yourself in the dark, though, is to take yourself outdoors, where, as David Whyte says in his poem 'Sweet Darkness', 'The night will give you a horizon / further than you can see.'

CHAPTER 2

Tools of the Trade

I go to Nature to be soothed and healed,
and to have my senses put in tune once more.

JOHN BURROUGHS

Sometimes we forget that despite coming into the world as bare-naked infants, Mother Nature nevertheless has designed us perfectly to thrive on planet Earth. Our capacity to invent and develop tools and hunting weapons enabled past generations to live more comfortably, but I want to emphasise the biological specifications we come equipped with from birth, rather than any requirement to go shopping. We take these attributes – our human senses – very much for granted.

Understanding our senses helps us gain more from our exploration of the dark. The richer the harvest, the deeper the connection. This is why it's worth giving our attention to each of our primary senses: to understand how we can increase our capacity and confidence at night, and, for that matter, by the hours of daylight too.

There are also technological aids that offer extra possibilities on a night-walk, especially for nature educators, and I discuss the use of binoculars and bat detectors, for example, in this chapter as well.

Our Sensory Equipment

How many senses do human beings have? Five, right?

Well, yes and no. Sight, touch, smell, hearing and taste are the commonly known senses, but if we consider that the basic function of our senses is to react to stimulation, we can extend their scope wider, perhaps, than we think.

With an information-gathering function as the criterion, clearly we possess many more senses than 'the big five'. For example, our sense of balance is not something we can see, hear, smell, taste or feel, but it is very important information for the brain to process, as anyone who has tried to walk a tightrope or balance beam, or even a straight line under the influence of too much alcohol, can testify. Other faculties help us gather information about direction, time, spatial awareness, hunger and thirst. Then there is the intriguing, precognitive 'sixth sense': our intuition. Most people can relate to their own experience of this, a time when they had a 'sense of something about to happen', before it actually does happen. Apparently, this precognitive capacity is more developed in some people than others.

A final clearly distinguishable sense is that awareness we have of our well-being, or in its absence, our sense of 'dis-ease'.

I have not found any definitive account quantifying the number of senses, but most researchers think there are between nine and twenty-one senses, depending on how they are defined. Certainly, there are a lot more than five.

However, in terms of being outdoors at night, it makes more 'sense' to focus on some of the tangible senses such as sight, hearing, smell and touch, and how to employ them as our 'tools of the trade'. We can also improve our capacity to sharpen our senses, which will enable us to get closer to nocturnal nature. So, let's visit these four main senses in turn to glean some useful information.

Sight

For the ancient Greeks, the eye was not a mere passive instrument to receive light and image as modern science would have it. One of the main theories, advocated by great thinkers such as Plato and Ptolemy, proposed instead that there was a 'pale light' that went forth from the eye and then returned with its harvest from the world, as a traveller might bear gifts. This appeals to my sense of poetry, and to my experience of the effect of night-time excursions. Our sight is certainly activated by the dark, as we strain to discern its costumes, characters and components. More than this, we can all testify to the insights and perspectives that the night-time affords us. Our eyes therefore perceive things we cannot grasp by the light of day, as Theodore Roethke wrote:

In a dark time, the eye begins to see.

Take a straw poll in any group of people, asking them, 'Which of your senses would you choose to keep, if you had to lose the rest?' In my experience, the majority will vote in favour of sight. That reflects our status as a sight-dominated species – the loss of sight isolates us more than any other type of sensory deprivation. Our language reflects this as well; think of all the phrases that link understanding with sight. 'I see what you mean' to 'throw light upon something' and 'the light came on in my brain'. Not to mention verbs like 'reflect', 'illustrate' and 'illuminate'.

Thinking in biological terms, a partnership evolved in humans between the senses of hearing and sight to enable successful hunting. Tracing back to our early ancestors, when we began shifting our centre of gravity by standing upright on two legs, we became less dependent on our sense of smell, relying more upon our eyes for the sighting of both predators and prey, especially as forest gave way to savannah and much more open country.

When working with a group of children, I often ask them to tell me how many eyes they have. After a few puzzled expressions as they consider whether this is a trick question, the answer arrives. 'Two.' That prompts the next enquiry: 'Why has nature given us two? What can you do with two eyes, that is difficult with one?' We then distinguish the advantage of binocular vision, in particular for measuring distances and giving us the sense of perspective.

Next I connect the chain of questions to our biology. 'Where are your eyes?' I ask, again receiving confused looks in return. (The questions have very obvious answers, but in the asking, they invite us to consider them in a new light.) 'The front of our heads – yes! What other animals also have eyes in the front, and what links us to them?' Once we have generated a list of mammals like foxes, weasels, dogs, cats, etc., and birds of prey, we can easily categorise ourselves as belonging to the predator class, albeit with omnivorous characteristics.

It's surprising how many children need reminding of our animal nature, and it's healthy to challenge our presumptions of our superiority over the animal kingdom, with a few home truths about how our basic biology developed from our hunter-gatherer past. We may not be able to see as far as a kestrel, which can clearly distinguish a beetle from 50 metres (164 feet) away, but our eyes can take in distant horizons as well as focus on objects at close quarters, and in that they are a highly versatile asset.

We also take it for granted that most of us see the world in glorious Technicolor. And what a pleasure it is, too, to be able to appreciate colours – imagine if the world was monochrome, how diminished life would be.

Vision is a complex sense, which involves the brain interpreting signals from the eyes. In humans, there are two types of photoreceptor cells concentrated at the back of the eyeball, in the retina. The retina, contains two types of light receptor cells, *cones* and *rods*. Cones are responsible for us being able to see in colour and perceive things in bright light, whereas cones function best in low light levels, allowing us to see in dim light.

There are several cone types, with particular sensitivities to different light wavelengths. The brain combines the signals from each cone type to 'see' colour. This is a bit like mixing primary paint colours to achieve all the colours of the rainbow. The more cone types a species has, the wider its range of colour perception. Mammals tend to have two or three cone types. Certain animals, such as cats, dogs and rabbits, have a poor range of colour vision. Their eyes contain cone cells that are sensitive to blue and green light, and so they tend to see a spectrum of mostly greys, blues and yellows. Other animals, however, have a broader spectrum of colour at their disposal – monkeys, ground squirrels, birds, insects, and many fish.

In terms of the animal kingdom, we humans perceive a wider spectrum of colour than most animals. The presence of extra cones that are also sensitive to red light enhances our range of colour vision. Perhaps this advantage has more of a cultural value to us than a basic survival function, though subtle shades of colouring aid us in diagnosing the ripeness of fruit or vegetables, the toxic nature of berries and can even help pinpoint the whereabouts of prey or predators.

Eagles have vision in the super-sense category and can spot a mouse a mile below, whilst a sloth is so dim-sighted it has trouble seeing any animal that isn't moving. Then there are those with specialist capacities like bees and butterflies that perceive colours that we cannot. In their case, ultraviolet patterns in the leaves of the plants they pollinate help guide the insects to the plants' blossoms.

When it comes to the invertebrate world, there is simply too much variety to categorise. Generally speaking, spiders have eight eyes and poor vision, whilst some flies have thousands of tiny lenses in their compound eyes, and near-360-degree vision. Ah, that explains why it's so difficult to sneak up on a fly!

The eyes of diurnal animals – those that are active during the day – contain a higher proportion of cones, which enables excellent perception of colour with high visual acuity in daylight. Most nocturnal animals have eyes with an abundance of rods but relatively few cones. This makes for excellent low-light vision but, conversely, can compromise daylight vision. Most mammals have more rods than cones in their retina, and these cells are generally situated towards the outer perimeter. Rods detect movement, rather than shape and colour, and so are critical for peripheral vision.

Peripheral Vision

Seeing 'out of the corner of your eye' is the way we often describe peripheral vision, and when it comes to getting close to wildlife, it's well worth paying attention to this part of your vision. (For a neat little activity to measure the range of your peripheral vision, see 'Hawk Eyes' in chapter 3 on page 29.)

Peripheral vision is weaker in humans than in most other mammals, but it is possible to improve it. Pilots, for example, train their peripheral vision to search for aircraft when dark.

By practising this focus on what you can see out of the corner of your eyes, it's possible to bring more and more details to your attention. And our ability to discern slight movements and/or changes in the patterns of the natural world will bring us closer to the wildlife we are hopeful of seeing. Whether during the day or at night, we often first catch the movement of animals or birds in the corner of our eyes, and then bring it into the centre of our vision.

You could try this now, or at anytime with your family or group. Stare straight ahead, and see what movement you can detect using your peripheral vision. If it's a summer's day, you will probably easily discern some insects flitting through the air, or if there is a breeze, you may see movement in the treetops.

Another way to improve your field of vision is to practice juggling. In order to juggle you must place your focus on a specific mid-air point and use the information from your peripheral vision to judge your catches successfully. We've all been amazed by the consummate skill of jugglers at the top of their game, whose feats of dexterity and precision require extraordinary levels of peripheral vision, and all of whom achieved it by practising.

Night Vision

As explained above, the rod-shaped cells in our eyes allow us to see shapes and movement in dim light and help us navigate through the dark; cone-shaped cells require more light to activate. For this reason you might notice that you don't see colour in the dark; instead, everything appears in shades of grey. Switch on a light, however, and the retina's cones activate, relaying colour information to the brain. Most of our cones are concentrated in the centre of the retina, which provides us with our sharp-focused vision of what is in front of us, especially in good light conditions. In contrast, most of the rods are located in around the edges of our retina. This is why you can see things better in your peripheral vision at night.

These days we often encounter the dark in a sudden change, such as when we step from inside a brightly lit house and into the night outdoors. The night will seem profoundly dark when we do this, because our 'night eyes' are not yet functioning properly. In order to maximise our night vision potential, it's best to allow our eyes time to adjust to the dark. If that is done slowly by avoiding any bright, artificial light through dusk and into the dark, then we will be well prepared.

If, however, our night eyes are exposed to bright light, then a light-sensitive pigment called rhodopsin in the rod cells bleaches and it loses its functionality of assisting with low-light vision. It then takes thirty to forty minutes in the dark for rhodopsin to regenerate fully, although most of the recovery occurs within the first five to ten minutes. Vitamin A is needed for your body to synthesise rhodopsin, and vitamin A is converted from beta-carotene, which is abundant in carrots – so there's real science behind that old wives tale…

Given the chance, our capacity for seeing in the dark is greater than we would think. It's also true to say that our night vision is not as developed as that of some animals, particularly those adapted to hunt and forage at night. This is usually to do with differences in anatomy, such as having larger eyes, a greater dilation of the iris or a greater number of rod cells.

Cats and dogs have evolved to be superbly designed for nocturnal hunting. Their eyes have a high density of rods and they can see perfectly well with as little as 15 per cent of the light levels that humans would need.

Hearing

Whilst we can recognise the limitations of our sense of hearing in comparison to many other animals, we nevertheless have a highly developed sense of hearing, and it should not be underestimated in our quest to get closer to wildlife.

In particular, where our vision is obscured, like in a forest, our ears must become our eyes, 'seeing' what our vision cannot detect. It's an old hunters' maxim to 'see with your ears'. Birds, for example, are more often heard before they are seen, and many are not seen at all in the canopy. In fact, it's true that generally wildlife is heard before it is seen. By paying particular attention to what we hear, we will be informed about what to look for. For example, we hear a rustle in the canopy above and we know instinctively where to look to find it. The placement of our ears on either side of the head means we can calculate approximate distance and direction, in a split second too. If we had only one functional ear, our hearing would be a lot less accurate and we'd struggle to locate wildlife through sound alone.

Of course, our sense of hearing plays a wider, significant role in our cultural, spiritual and emotional lives. Our emotional memory is triggered when we hear a piece of music from our past. Immediately we can connect it to a particular time and place. We are moved, inspired, affected by music like no other species (with the possible exception of our cetacean cousins, whales and dolphins, that have delightfully been discovered to possess complex communication capacity through sound). It seems counterintuitive, but sound travels faster through denser mediums, so it travels faster in water than air. If you have climbed at altitude, you can likely testify to the slower movement of sound up where the air is less dense.

> *I am hearing all the secret whisperings of the world!*
> *... I is hearing the little ants chittering to each other*
> *as they scuddle around in the soil. ... I is sometimes*
> *hearing far away music coming from the stars in*
> *the sky.*　　　　**ROALD DAHL**, *The BFG*

Our hearing is tightly bound in with our communication with each other, and in the context of education, many of us who have an aural learning style will learn best through our ears rather than our eyes.

It's also a common experience that our other senses are heightened when we are deprived of one or more. I once tried wearing a blindfold for three consecutive days and nights. Being blindfolded dramatically changed my experience of daily life, primarily through the medium of sound. My listening abilities seemed to grow exponentially; I felt a deeper intimacy with the world in general, and in particular with those people I came into contact with.

Needless to say, at night our hearing is keener, and with the noise of the day subsiding, more subtle or distant sounds of nocturnal nature can be captured, such as the rustle of foraging badgers, hoots of territorial tawny owls, mating foxes or churring nightjars.

When we step off the beaten trail into an unfamiliar environment like a woodland, our imagination heightens our sense of hearing as we fantasise about all the unseen things that might lurk in the shadows to pounce on us. A little dose of fear makes us very alert – the primeval feeling arising from the realisation we might not be at the top of the food chain. Even if there are no longer predators to hunt us in our woods and fields, our bodies register the potential threat of something leaping out of the dark to surprise us.

This was made clearest to me on a wilderness youth exchange programme to the Kalahari Desert with an unlikely group of British, Russians and Batswana in the 1980s. The wildlife warden suggested we 'experience' the forest on our own for a while. So he walked us in a (very) large circle around our makeshift camp, dropping us off one by one until we were alone with the instruction to sit for a while and then find our way back to camp. In this forest we knew that lions and hyaenas hunted, together with baboons, snakes and leopards. This knowledge, and the prospect of encountering elephants, put our senses onto their highest possible alert. On a scale of one to ten, I reckon mine were on twelve as I sat, sweated and then stalked my way back in the direction of where I hoped camp would be. I was unexpectedly alone in unfamiliar terrain with none of the literacy of the native people, and I felt *scared.* My fear was mixed up with adrenaline, though, and I'd never felt so juicily alive!

I have seen a similar effect on countless nightwalks in Britain with groups of children, and adults, too, exploring in either unfamiliar or familiar terrain. Away from the anaesthetising effects of streetlights, television and central heating, plenty of fears are projected out into the dark.

When I lead a nightwalk, I light my lantern in the forest and invite everyone to take their sit mat and walk away from the light, as far as they dare go, and then sit and experience the forest in as much darkness as they can abide, for twenty minutes or so. The flickering candle flame offers reassurance to those who remain in view of it, and guides everyone back in when I give the owl-call signal.

The impact of that experience is clear as we then share our stories of startling cries and mysterious rustlings of nocturnal nature, or of the deepest quiet ever experienced, or of the fear and excitement of sitting alone in the darkness, in a forest. Another big life experience to chalk off. 'Good medicine', too, I reckon.

To illustrate further the deeper listening that's always available to us, here is a strange little story of disorientation and, er... underpants! One summer I was camping alone in a dense Devon forest on a moonless night and I awoke in the early hours in need of a pee. Stumbling out into the deep dark, still half-asleep, I walked a few paces and achieved my objective. I turned and staggered back to the tent. Except that the tent had gone!

The darkness was so complete I could not make out the tent's pointed silhouette. After wandering about waving my arms in front of me for a bit, I stopped to take in the situation.

What to do? I was facing the very real prospect of wandering about until I found some habitation, where I would have to knock at the door to ask for assistance from someone, in my underpants.

I was now very wide awake and very present to both the gravity and comedy of my predicament. Instinctively I crouched, slowed my breathing, softened my lower jaw and began to listen, deeply. I was going to have to 'hear' my way back home. The silence of this particular night turned out to be to my advantage. After a while I could discern a very subtle, regular rhythm – the faintest of faint 'ticking' sound – and my tiny alarm clock guided me in. Phew!

A cautionary tale to remind us that there is potentially always another layer of sound beneath the surface of what we hear; we just need to listen more deeply. By actively 'reaching' further and further with our listening, we become better oriented and hear more. Hunters all over the world know this, from the San who learn and practise imitations of birds and animals to help them gain proximity to those using the modern technology of digital hearing aids to capture more sound in their quest for game.

One of the non-technological ways we can instantly locate this 'under-layer' of sound is to employ our very own 'deer ears' – see the Deer Ears activity on page 30.

Smell

As with the sense of sight, there are many idioms about the sense of smell, like 'I smell a rat', 'something fishy going on' or 'something doesn't smell right'; figurative expressions that equate the sense of smell to the ability to intuitively discern trouble or obfuscation. It is a sense we can trust then, unlike the vagaries of our sight, which can play tricks on us through optical illusion.

Perhaps the scent equivalent of an optical illusion is the way we fail to notice the smells we are most accustomed to. The best example is our home environment, which to us doesn't have any odour at all, of course. But, any time you visit someone else's house, there's no doubt you can immediately detect a smell resonance that is uniquely theirs.

By the same measure, we know it's possible to acclimatise to very unpleasant smells, as those living near an industrial outlet will testify to. However, there is a nearly universal human response to the smell of something foul: a grimace and/or expletives! This is a basic biological survival mechanism, to let ourselves and others know something is not safe to ingest.

To save you the time and trouble counting, I can tell you that on average we inhale twenty-three thousand times per day. This is a lot of olfactory information for our brain to process. It's not just the rich texture of experience that our capacity to smell gives us, it's also the invisible dangers we are exposed to if we cannot perceive them through sight. The strongest smells we are likely to encounter in an average day are to do with toilets or rotting food. The latter in particular are in a category we could call life-threatening. We barely register what we are doing as we sniff the milk or yoghurt to see if it's gone off. Generally speaking, we are quite confident of what's still edible. This is a particular virtue of our sense of smell, to detect danger in the absence of any visual prompt or evidence. For example, mould we can see growing on a piece of food corroborates what our nose tells us; but even when we can't see any decay, we still trust our nose. Likewise, we would rely on our sense of smell to detect a gas leak or an unseen fire. Pity those with a condition known as anosmia, which deprives them of a sense of smell, either temporarily or permanently.

So far so obvious. But there's a lot more going on beneath.

The human nose can distinguish thousands of different smells and the sense of smell can trigger not only physical responses, but also memory and emotion. People tend to associate certain aromas or odours with particular times, people and places they have known, both positive and negative. And what about the intimacy of smells between people? It is said we choose our partners on the basis of a contrasting smell to our own, rather than a similar smell, and that this is a significant part of the selection process.

There are thousands of discernments we can make to distinguish between smells. In the 1950s British biochemist, John Amoore, created a classification system to organise odours into eight categories based on their molecular structure. These are: floral, ethereal, earthy, pungent, putrid, musky, camphor and peppermint. Although it remains a challenge to assimilate smells into neat categories that everyone agrees on, Amoore's are still used to classify odours in a general way.

For the animal kingdom, not unlike for ourselves, smell and scent are dominant in the pursuit of food, sex or recognition between family groups. The chemoreceptors in the nose are connected to the olfactory bulb in the brain, and the larger the bulb the more important the sense of smell is to that animal.

In terms of our quest to maximise our wildlife encounters during a nightwalk, our sense of smell is not as applicable as others, but learning about the olfactory abilities of some nocturnal creatures may help us to strategise how best to approach them.

The prime mover on the night stage here is the badger, with a sense of smell as acute as a dog's. In fact, it is thought that the badger's sense of smell might be as much as eight hundred times better than ours. The superiority of its sense of smell is evidenced in its skull. If you find a skull whilst out exploring the woods, look inside the nasal cavity. If it has a large opening, it's likely a badger skull.

With this understanding of how keen a badger's sense of smell is, it would therefore follow to be extra cautious about sending our own body odour towards badgers we are hoping to watch. It's best to avoid wearing highly fragrant antiperspirants or perfumes, and it's also important to position yourself downwind. (For more about this handsome night forager, see About Badgers on page 88.)

Touch

Unless at a fancy-dress party, we don't wear the whiskers of a cat and we certainly don't possess the sensitive eye-socket feathers of an owl to feel our way through the woods at night. But we do have a whole 2 square metres (22 square feet) of skin wrapped around our bodies, and that translates to approximately 5 million sensory receptors to help us meet and connect with our surroundings.

The most relevant aspect of touch in acquainting ourselves with nocturnal nature is feeling the breeze on our skin to determine wind direction. You might simply try turning around in a circle to see if you can feel the wind on your face, or, if only a gentle breeze is present, try licking your finger and sticking it up in the air – the side that turns cool indicates where the breeze is coming from. Properly detecting the wind direction can make all the difference to a successful encounter with a badger and some other types of wildlife, so don't forget to consult your skin organ for the relevant information. Sitting with your back to the wind and watching a badger sett will usually result in a long wait and a disappointing return on your investment.

The sense of touch can also play a role on those occasions in the lunar cycle when no moon means no light, or at least not enough photons for our ocular equipment to take advantage of, particularly under the canopy of the forest. At those times, is it possible for us to 'feel' our way down the path? We might envy the manatee here for its body covering of tiny sensory hairs that can extend its 'reach' in the waters in which it dwells.

We possess no such physical attributes, but we do seem predisposed to an extra sense that extends beyond our physical boundaries. As a student in the creative cauldron of the theatre rehearsal room, I recall experimenting with blindfold exercises to explore these boundaries in which I tried to sense how close a partner was, or walked towards a wall and sensed the right moment to stop. It was revealing how much 'information' we were able to gather in these risky exercises, helping us to improve our spatial awareness by cultivating that 'extra sense'. (And, by the way, nobody came to any harm.) In chapter 3, there are blindfold games and exercises to help heighten this acute awareness.

Another phenomenon that supports this capacity of ours is the sensation of 'phantom touch.' Think of the sensation that you feel when you've been wearing a hat for a long time and then remove it. Even after you take off the hat, it feels as though it's still on your head.

In our excursions into the deep dark, this sensing of our way down the path retains our night-cloak advantage. It's also a rather thrilling ride, demanding our full focus and attention. On countless nightwalks I have guided in the British countryside, I always issue an invitation to switch off the torches and go into 'stealth mode' to discover the possibilities of travelling in secrecy. Assuming that fear does not overwhelm the explorer, it's an instructive and rich experience of the night.

Sensory Exercises

I love leading simple exercises to help people 'get in the zone' for paying better attention in the outdoors. Wildlife has evolved in a context of the very old game of predator–prey and so tends to be discreet, either camouflaged by day or active under the cover of darkness. The lovely attunements I describe here are a way of extra-priming the senses to discern the subtle presence of nocturnal creatures.

As a general rule in sensory attunement, diminishing one sense tends to heighten others. Thus, some of these exercises work with sensory deprivation to sharpen our awareness. As the old saying about audiences in the theatre goes, 'The better the quality of attention, the better the quality of the performance.' It's just as true in the theatre of the natural world, and the best attention gains maximum results when it comes to getting closer to wildlife.

SENSE MEDITATION

To begin, ask the group to settle into whatever position you would like them to be in. This could be seated or standing, as long as they are not touching – an 'elbow's length' is perfect.

Equipment required:
None
Ages: 8 and up
Number of participants:
2–30

Then lead the group with your voice through the activity. Pause for a minute after each instruction to give the group time to take in sensations. For an adult group, the pauses can stretch a little longer, but no more than 2 minutes or you risk losing their attention and focus. Follow along the lines of this suggested script:

- Take a few moments to centre yourself. Close your eyes and pay attention to your breathing. Imagine your feet are roots going down into the earth and your body is like the trunk of a tree.
- Orientate yourself to the four cardinal directions (north, east, south and west). Point to where you think north is.
- Can you feel any breeze on your skin? Be aware of any other sensations on your skin, perhaps from the clothes you are wearing. Notice the physical contact point you have with the ground – what sensation do you have through this?
- Bring your attention to what you can hear. Listen for the furthest sound you can hear.
- Now listen for the closest sound.
- Listen for sounds coming from each of the four directions around you.
- Without opening your eyes, bring to mind some detail of your surroundings. Can you visualise the colours of the clothing worn by the person to your right? 'See' as much of the world around you as you can recall, relying on your visual memory.
- Open your eyes, and spend a minute with all your senses. Notice how your awareness has become more acute.

- Now you can check how much visually you remembered. Did you recall the details of what your neighbour was wearing? How about the direction of north – did you point the right way?

HAWK EYES

This exercise is a test of your range of peripheral vision. It's called Hawk Eyes because of the extraordinary capacities of raptors to locate prey from great distances.

Ask the group to spread themselves at least arm's length apart from each other. Instruct them to extend their arms straight in front of their bodies and point their two index fingers skywards.

Equipment required:
None
Ages: 6 and up
Number of participants:
2–30

Next, ask them to look into the distance between their two upraised fingers, preferably focusing on a distant object like a tree.

Tell them to slowly move their arms apart, keeping them straight and at eye level, wiggling those raised fingers so that their peripheral vision can detect the movement. Encourage them to continue until they have spread their arms to the point where they can just barely see those fingers in the 'corners' of their eyes whilst still looking straight ahead. Even when our eyes are fixed upon a distant point, we can still keep our wiggling fingers in our peripheral vision until they reach the edge of our range.

Notes

Explain that this is the broad range of human vision and it's surprising how far it extends. We have, as humans, about 150 degrees of peripheral vision per eye. But the visual field has been measured at 181 degrees in some people, which technically, I suppose, is seeing 'behind' you! People who wear glasses will notice that their range is slightly restricted when they try this exercise.

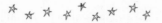

DEER EARS

This very effective little exercise will amplify the sounds around us, simply by 'growing' the size of our ears. We can then 'reach' further with our hearing to record what our eyes cannot find – especially helpful in the forest where the trees obscure our view.

Ask the group to cup their hands behind their ears. Demonstrate how to sculpt the hands to avoid gaps in the fingers. Suggest that the group close their eyes as this seems to focus our attention better to capture the sounds.

Equipment required:
None
Ages: 6 and up
Number of participants:
2–30

Tell the group members to orientate themselves to a constant sound, such as the wind in the trees, running water or distant traffic. Tell them to listen with 'deer ears' in place and then drop their hands to listen without. Give them time to switch repeatedly so they can fully appreciate the contrast in volume when they add their deer ears.

Next, ask the group members to turn their backs to the sound they are listening to. They should immediately notice how much less capacity they have to hear the sound. Show them how to place their cupped hands in front of their ears, with the 'cup' facing backwards, to capture and amplify the sound from behind.

COUNT THE SOUNDS

By individually accounting for each sound we can hear, we take much more notice of what's around us. In this simple activity, participants will record everything that is making a sound, even if it cannot be seen.

Start by asking the group to form a circle. This exercise is best done with everyone lying down on their backs, for maximum effect. If conditions are wet or muddy, however, then the group can remain standing.

Ask them to close their eyes, keep still and listen. (In order for this exercise to succeed, it's important to minimise sounds such as the shuffling of feet or noisy waterproofs.)

Their task is to count the number of different sounds they can hear and to tally each sound using their fingers. Give them about one minute to listen and count sounds.

Ask the group to then open their eyes, and if lying down, to sit up. Then ask them to raise up their hands in silence to reveal the number of sounds recorded. (Doing it this way, rather than asking for the number to be shouted out, reduces the pressure to compete with higher and higher numbers to impress the leader.) As so often with leading activities, the detail is significant in determining the success.

> **Equipment required:**
> None
> **Ages:** 6 and up
> **Number of participants:**
> 2–30

Next, ask for what they recorded, so that as a group you can make a list of every sound the group captured; usually, many more sounds are gathered collectively than any one individual would manage.

Finally, ask the group how many of those sounds can they see. After a few moments looking around, the group will report back that almost none of the sounds are observable, which serves to emphasise the importance of hearing.

BLOODHOUND

Start by asking an assistant to lay out a short trail about 5 metres (15 feet) long on the ground, using a substance that has a very distinct smell, for example vinegar or an essential oil like peppermint or tea tree. This can be done by applying the pungent substance to a rag, then

> **Equipment required:**
> 2 blindfolds
> Vinegar and/or some
>   essential oils
> Rags
> Sticks or ground pegs
> **Ages:** 8 and up
> **Number of participants:**
> 2 per trail (any number
>   of trails can be laid)

tying the rag to your foot and then stamping your way over open ground to establish a trail.

Choose two people to be 'bloodhounds' and blindfold them. Challenge the bloodhounds to attempt to follow the trail, on all fours with their noses to the ground, marking the trail as they go by placing sticks or ground pegs in the ground. The odours will dissipate quickly, especially on a hot day, and so set the bloodhounds on the trail without delay.

For a more advanced challenge, ask two helpers to simultaneously lay out two separate trails of contrasting smells, making sure the two trails cross at some point. Set a pair of bloodhounds to follow each trail, and watch what ensues when one trail crosses over the other. Inevitably there might be some confusion at the point of intersection, but that is the point of the challenge, and this also leads to some of the fun and enjoyment of the exercise. (Detecting the odour trail is slow work, so there is no danger of anyone getting hurt, even if two bloodhounds accidentally collide.)

PASS THE SMELL

This exercise takes its cue from the fact that there are at least eight general categories of smell commonly observed (as was discussed on page 25). Prepare in advance for this activity by placing a small amount of twelve different fragrant materials separately into the bottles.

Equipment required:
12 small bottles – without labels, numbered from 1–12
Fragrant items, such as essential oils and spices
Optional – Blindfolds
Ages: 11 and up
Number of participants: 6–20

Ask the group to sit in a circle and begin passing bottles around the ring, instructing the group to take a sniff to identify each smell, but to keep their guess to themselves. You can pass bottles in both directions to engage everyone more quickly.

Once all the bottles have completed the circuit and are back in your possession, ask for their guesses as to the definitive list of smells.

Notes

Smells that will stimulate the palette work well, such as rose, lemon, mint, lavender, ginger and pepper. Include a pungent or acrid example like vinegar, and soy sauce is also a good one to test everyone's smell-memory. Don't miss the opportunity for a bit of reaction provided by something putrid like a rotten egg or manure!

BAREFOOT WALK

For a Barefoot Walk (also called Nightline by some activity leaders) a rope tied between and around trees creates a 'handrail' to follow. Holding onto the rope helps participants feel secure and keep their balance, allowing them to immerse themselves in exquisite sensory exploration as bare feet contact the Earth, soil and humus.

Set up the handrail in advance; the terrain must not be threatening so that people can go barefoot without fear of puncture wounds.

Start by explaining that each person will be following the rope in turn. Invite participants to take off their shoes and socks, because it will increase the sensory experience.

> **Equipment required:**
> 1 rope, 15–25 metres
> (50–80 feet) long
> Blindfolds (optional)
> Natural objects
> (optional, see Notes
> and Variants)
> **Ages:** 11 and up
> **Number of participants:**
> 4–12

Appoint at least two helpers to manage 'traffic flow'.

One by one, call people forward to start travelling along the rope. To avoid 'traffic jams', send those who have opted to keep their shoes on down the trail first, because they will tend to move more quickly. Allow at least 2 metres (7 feet) between participants.

Notes and Variants

Wearing a blindfold dramatically heightens the experience and means this can also become a 'nocturnal activity' during the daylight hours.

As an extra embellishment, gather some natural objects in advance, such as skulls, feathers, shells and bones. Tie each item to the rope at intervals for people to explore with their fingertips. This has the added bonus of slowing things down.

TREE ID

This is a good old-fashioned guessing game based on a sensory impression of twigs and leaves from contrasting species of trees – try to get them from both evergreen and deciduous trees.

To begin, ask the group to sit in a circle and close their eyes.

Pass the twigs and leaves around the circle. Encourage everyone to spend time getting to know each one through their sense of touch, making acquaintance with the differences between each species. This is best done in silence.

> **Equipment required:**
> 5 sets of twigs/leaves
>   from 5 species of tree
> Piece of cloth, 1 square
>   metre (10 square feet)
> **Ages:** 11 and up
> **Number of participants:**
> 4–12

When all the twigs and leaves have made the circuit back to you, hide them under a cloth and ask the group to open their eyes and play a game of 'identify the species'. Explain that their task is to name, in the correct order, the five species they explored. Each time a correct guess is made, you can bring out the relevant item for them to see.

Notes and Variants

If you suspect there is little knowledge about trees in your group, then identifying the five species of trees first on a walk might be good preparation for the activity.

PRINT ID

In advance, use the boots to make three clear tread impressions in some mud. Note that the mud needs to be a firm consistency in order for it not to be altered during the exercise. Make as many sets of prints as needed to accommodate the size of your group.

With eyes closed, the challenge is for participants to explore the prints with their fingertips to see whether they can distinguish the different patterns of tread as well as distinguishing left feet from right.

> **Equipment required:**
> 3 boots, each wih a dif-
> ferent tread pattern
> **Ages:** 14 and up
> **Number of participants:**
> 3–6 for each set
> of prints

After they have explored each print, challenge them to see if they can match up each boot with its track in the mud.

Finally, with their eyes open, they can explore the prints again to see which ones they got right.

'Technical' Tools

Now we have considered our innate capacities of wildlife detection through our own sensory equipment, let's turn our attention to technological aids to help us get closer to nocturnal nature.

Torches

'Let there be light', and thanks to the dizzying array of torches available, there will always be light in the darkness. Gone are the days when only a big and bulky torch with chunky batteries had the power to reach far into the dark to spot things in the distance. Nowadays, with a mere pocket-sized, handheld torch, it's possible to send a powerful beam into the trees to spot a tawny owl, or across the meadow to see a herd of fallow deer. Such torches have a zoom effect, focusing a smaller laser beam of light to pinpoint a subject of interest.

Many head torches have powerful beams, too, though they are less effective at focusing a beam of light, and tend to spread their light fairly wide. However, many of them come equipped with an option to switch to a red light. This is particularly useful to maintain a discreet presence when wanting to get close to nocturnal mammals who, through some biological shortcoming, do not register a red spectrum of vision. It conveniently permits you to see, without being seen. White light, by contrast will disrupt your own night vision as well as compromising the vision of mammals you are hoping to watch, whereas red light will be non-invasive. A red filter can easily be attached to a handheld torch, too, if it does not come equipped with this facility.

Bear in mind, with torches it's not a case of 'one size fits all'. When you're planning after-dark activities, it's better to bring one that will provide a long-range illumination, as well as one that will also enable observation at close quarters.

Binoculars

It may surprise you to learn that binoculars are on the nightwalk equipment list. In terms of seeing more in the dark, though, binoculars are an asset. Their obvious employment is for moon or planet gazing, but I recommend you also use them 'on the ground', for wildlife viewing, and here's why…

By day, the combination of lenses in a pair of binoculars work together to magnify and gather in distant images for close-up viewing. By night, those same lenses act to funnel in all the available light, concentrating it into a narrow focus and enhancing our night vision.

This works best when your eyes are already accustomed to the dark, and can be an invaluable aid to discerning the shapes and movement of nocturnal creatures like deer or badgers.

In terms of wildlife watching, the general recommendation is to choose binoculars with the appropriate ratio of aperture (the size of the lens opening) and magnification (the power of the lens). The formula is to multiply the aperture number by five. The closer that number is to the magnification figure, the better for wildlife viewing. For example, a pair of 8 × 40 binoculars would offer the perfect ratio, because 8 (the aperture) times 5 equals 40 (the magnification). A pair of 7 × 50 would be more unbalanced.

It's tempting to plump for the biggest magnification, assuming that this will gain the best image, but such binoculars can become heavy and thus harder to hold steady, not to mention being less convenient to carry.

Bat Detectors

Bats hunt using a remarkably efficient system of making high-frequency calls and following the sound waves that are returned to them, much like an echo, hence why this process is called echolocation. The sounds they make vary according to species size and weight.

The issue with bats, however, is that they are very small, very dark and very silent, at least for our hearing range. Not a very promising set of conditions for encountering them at night, unless you are outside at early dusk in the summertime, when it's possible to see them in flight before they are obscured by darkness.

Locating bats at night therefore requires some help from technology. And the moment when you bring out the exciting-sounding 'bat detector' from your nightwalk bag is a sweet one. We all love a bit of tech – even more so if it's in the service of something good, like bat conservation.

The bat-detecting machine is a simple concept and there are varying degrees of technical complexity depending what your interest is. The range and diversity of models has grown exponentially. There are specialist types of detector for the professionals and 'bat nerds' that will distinguish between every species with some precision, and make recordings of their sounds for later analysis. Or, there are the simple 'frequency division' variety that do a basic job of 'translating' the sounds bats are making to a lower frequency that we can hear.

Overall, there are three different types of detector on the market and for the amateur enthusiast the frequency division detectors will do just fine. Time expansion detectors are for recording and analysing bat calls in much more detail, and as such are used for gathering field data in bat conservation. Heterodyne detectors will discern between species and the higher specification models will do this more accurately. But, 'You pays your money and you takes your choice,' as the old saying goes. For the purposes of introducing bats at night, and locating them through the sounds a bat detector captures, you only need a basic model, available for less than £100. In my career, I've used various iterations of the reliable Batbox brand of heterodyne detector, which introduces the idea of different frequencies produced by different species at an entry-level price for this type of detector and if you are looking to lead groups yourself. I have found these to be a good balance of cost, reliability and specification. See the Links and

Resources section on page 197 to help you navigate your way through the maze of products.

Perhaps I should take a step back to explain the rudiments of frequencies and sound waves, so that you can demystify the workings of a bat detector for a group on a nightwalk.

If you recall your physics lessons at school you'll remember that sounds travel in waves and the number of waves per second is the frequency; the more sound waves per second, the higher the frequency. The unit used to measure frequency is the hertz (Hz), so 1 Hz is equal to 1 wave per second (sometimes described as 1 cycle per second) and 1 kHz (1 kilohertz, which is 1,000 hertz) is equal to 1,000 waves per second.

The calls made by most European species of bats are ultrasonic, ranging between 20 kHz and 130 kHz. This means they are mostly beyond the frequency range of the human ear, which can reach close to 20 kHz. There are some exceptions, and bats in the roost can sometimes be heard making contact calls by those who have unimpaired hearing. It's worth noting that children can often detect sounds that adults cannot and women are also generally more able to pick up higher frequencies than men.

The technology of a bat detector in effect reduces the number of waves per second to produce a lower frequency and thereby make them audible to human ears. Calling these machines bat detectors rather limits their scope. Other creatures, such as shrews, also emit high frequency sounds, and bat detectors are also being used to analyse the stridulations of crickets and grasshoppers. These machines are directional and you will certainly pick up all sorts of other sounds if you point the detector at rustling clothes or footsteps in the long grass. Thus, they need to be used with a bit of care. On introducing the bat detector to a group, I will usually ask if anyone has a bunch of keys they could jingle, which is one way to show how it can pick up sounds from far away. The range varies on different models, but an average is 30 metres (100 feet), as long as you are pointing in the approximate direction of the flying bats.

For some practical advice and tips if you are considering purchasing a bat detector, you could do no better than attend some bat-watching events to see what the professionals and more experienced guides are using. You could then try them out for yourself to learn what will work best for you.

Get in touch with a local bat group to see if they run such events and/or perhaps attend a Bat Conservation Trust training session. And for tips on leading a session using a bat detector, see Bat Detecting on page 86.

Moth Traps

As with bat detectors, the widening choice of moth traps can be beguiling, but there are three general types to choose from, all of which require a 12V battery to operate.

The Robinson trap probably best suits the 'professionals', mostly because it offers 100 per cent retention for post-capture analysis. Its main drawbacks are that it is more expensive than other types and is bulky to transport.

The Skinner trap scores highly on price and portability, but does not retain the moths as well as the Robinson model.

The Heath trap is similarly lighter on price and weight, but it does not catch or retain as effectively as the other two.

Another option is to set up a 'moth tent' – which can also be bought or improvised – with an LED light inside. This makes observing the moths a group-friendly alternative. If you are improvising this from a normal camping tent, try using the inner part of the tent that is made of fine mesh rather than the flysheet, because the mesh can be more effective at emitting the light.

Home-fashioned alternatives are also a viable option, taking your design cues from some of the models above. As long as you have the right sort of light to attract the moths you can use all sorts of materials to create a safe-haven box for the moths. When I worked at the Devon Wildlife Trust, we used to use egg boxes, inside which the moths seemed to like resting.

The more enthusiastic or professional lepidopterists (people who study moths and butterflies) mostly use the 80–125 watt MV (mercury vapour) bulbs, but also effective are the gentler actinic bulb. This form of lighting uses a range of 15–40 watts, and is enough to attract the moths, but not annoy the neighbours. It's not so bright as the old mercury vapour lighting that was used extensively and effectively, but which is now being phased out as a hazardous substance.

Other Equipment

Extra accoutrements for nightwalks include night vision scopes, telescopes and various hearing amplification aids to enhance our capacities to see and hear even more accurately in the dark.

In my view, these devices are not especially useful for the sort of applications described in this book. It's not to say they are not more precise, accurate and effective than our own unaided human senses are. My objection is more that they add to the clutter and expense, and in terms of group use, they are not a very practical way of experiencing a nightwalk collectively. For individual excursions into the night-time realm, I dare say they have their use for getting even more intimate with the creatures. In particular, a telescope for stargazing is a wonderful addition, especially when there are cosmic events to behold like comets or the full moon, or some of the planets revealing themselves in the night sky.

For some more specific guidelines and possibilities in regard to this sort of specialist equipment, I refer you onto technical manuals and websites to understand their capacities and applications. (See the Links and Resources section on page 197.)

What to Wear

Don't underestimate the basic principle of getting dressed properly for spending time outdoors at night. Warm and/or waterproof clothing is the obvious prerequisite, given that the cold and wet can be a consistent feature of nocturnal excursions, even in summertime. It never ceases to surprise me how 'badly dressed' the British can be when it comes to dressing themselves for the outdoors, and I'm not referring to style here. This is emphasised by the all-too-common trend of parents who send their children on camp with insufficient or inefficient weatherproof clothing. It's one of the fundamentals of outdoor leadership to ensure the group is equipped to cope, and, if not, to either have spare clothing available or be prepared to adapt or change the plan. A shorter nightwalk that's enjoyable is preferable to an uncomfortable experience that might have the effect of putting the participants off for life. A judicious and discreet assessment of what people are wearing before setting out is always a good idea. And, needless to say, getting yourself dressed properly is key, so that your perceptions, sensibilities and decision-making are not adversely affected by your own discomfort.

Because nocturnal animals are so well-equipped in detecting any threatening presence, it's also worth ditching our fashion preoccupations for discreet, understated attire. There is an extra factor here to consider, which is the sounds your clothing makes. Certain fabrics are much noisier than others, and, ironically, typical weather-resistant clothing is the worst offender – and the very worst you could wear would be white or fluorescent waterproofs. Darker colours should be worn and military camouflage clothing is one of the cheapest, most readily available choices available. If you wish to spend the money, professional stalker's camouflage gear is very effective, but it is much more expensive than other outdoor clothing.

Cotton and wool are the quietest of materials to wear. Synthetic fabrics tend to rustle loudly as the fabric brushes past itself or against any undergrowth. The stalking process sometimes involves crawling along the ground or through dense bushes, and apart from the noise, these modern materials tend to tear more easily. A traditional thick, finely woven wool jacket is an ideal item to muffle sounds and offers general weatherproofing. If you can afford them, wax jackets have also been a constant favourite of deerstalkers and bird watchers as a durable, weatherproof option.

Regarding shoes and boots, look for footwear that won't give away your presence by its brightness, and footwear that is not big and clunky and difficult to move quietly in. The more you can 'feel' the ground in your shoes, the more quietly you can operate. The moccasins of the native peoples in America were worn like a second skin and helped the hunters move as silently as the wild creatures do.

As ever in the British climate, it's an equation of weather and terrain, and soft shoes aren't so appropriate in squelchy mud. Wellington boots are the other extreme, and are a low-cost option that can be used for wet and muddy conditions, but not advisable if there is climbing to be done. With a little more investment, there are softer and more comfortable wellington boots on the market which are an ideal compromise between comfort and concealment.

CHAPTER 3

Getting Attuned to the Dark

The world is full of magic things,
patiently waiting for our senses to grow sharper.

W.B. YEATS

I n the wild, there is an eternal conflict between the hunter and the hunted, and creatures have evolved over the millennia to be the victor in this deadly game. Whether predator or prey, wild creatures have found ways to remain unseen when needed and the dark is an ideal environment in which to conceal oneself. This means you'll need to attune your senses to the subtle qualities of the night-time world to uncover the nocturnal animals hidden by darkness. This chapter features activities and games to help a group 'get in the zone' for paying attention in the outdoors with heightened awareness and moving silently along a trail at night.

If your group is new to night-time activities, try some of these at dusk to start, before all daylight has faded away. Remember, for humans, the coming of night traditionally ushered in the fear and trepidation of known and unknown threats. In many ways, though, dusk is the richest time to be out and about, present for the fading light of day and the rising tide of darkness. It's a particularly fruitful time for observing wildlife; the air is heavy with anticipation (or is it trepidation?) and we can notice enhanced fragrances that the cooling Earth sends out to entice us into the dark.

Attunement Activities

Here are two activities designed to provide a direct, one-to-one experience of the outdoors at night. Your discretion as group leader will be required as to the use of torches during these activities. Relying on one's night vision can be a rich part of the experience for people as they walk through the darkness. But on some occasions, such as on darker nights, it will be appropriate to invite the responsible use of a torch to help people find their way.

SIT-SPOT

Sit alone outdoors for a short period of time at dusk or in the dark. That's the essence of this key activity, which works well in tandem with some of the silent movement games later in this chapter. It's a good way to begin the process of gaining confidence and becoming acquainted with the night.

Also called Anchor Point or Magic Spot, this activity invites us to be in a more direct and simple relationship with the natural world. Through daytime, this can be challenging enough, especially for those not used to being in wild nature, or even to being in their own company or sitting still for longer than a few minutes.

Equipment required:
Sit mats
Candle lantern
Torches (optional)
Ages: 8 and up
Number of participants:
2–30

I usually start with an enticement, asking the group to describe any wildlife encounters they have had. Their responses usually reveal a pattern of being on their own, or at least being quiet, at the time of the encounter. I follow this with an anecdote of my own about an animal encounter to illustrate and underline the importance of being still and quiet, and how a sit-spot is the very best way of maximising our chances to see and hear wildlife.

I then invite the group to each take a sit mat and to find a spot on their own for a period of time that is commensurate with my expectations of their capacity. Usually this is between 10–20 minutes for a group of children and 30–40 minutes for a group of adults.

I always bring along a candle lantern on nightwalks, and it works well for this activity. Once everyone has found their way to their spot, within sight of the lantern light, I explain that when everyone is settled I will extinguish the candle, so that we can experience the dusk or night fully. Then, when I relight it, it will be their signal to return.

A sit-spot in the twilight hours or darkness of night could be a step too far for younger children, or those who are not settled or self-contained. If this is the case, they can sit with a parent, teacher or friend, but with a sit-spot the aspiration is always for a solo experience, because sitting outdoors is qualitatively different when you are on your own. You are not distracted by the social process of another human; you are more attentive to your surroundings and therefore notice more activity from birds and animals. Solitude also leads us to a more thoughtful, reflective place, which is good for both physical and mental health.

CIRCLE WALK

A circle walk creates a container that allows the group to safely explore some solo time with some navigational simplicity. Offering this activity during the twilight hours might be preferable to the challenge of darkness. Judgement must be used as to when a group is ready for solo night navigation. Use your discretion – this activity is not meant to challenge unduly.

Walk the group in a wide circle around a predetermined

Equipment required:
Torches (optional)
Ages: 11 and up
Number of participants:
6–30

central point, for example the campfire or base camp. Drop them off one by one, spaced apart equidistant from each other around the circumference of the circle you are walking. How far away from the central point you go will depend on the terrain and the capacities of the group. Ideally, the group members will not be able to see the central point of the circle from their drop-off spot. On a given signal, they simply make their way from their drop-off location back to the central point, using their 'night eyes' to find their way. Best if they can be given enough time to dwell, pause, linger and bathe in the night if they choose, rather than rushing back. Invite this to be part of the experience, and suggest they might take note when or if they stray out of their comfort zone in this activity, to reflect on later.

Use a signal, such as a whistle, for calling everybody back after a certain amount of time. The time you allow will be dictated by factors including the terrain, size of the circle, age range and group capacities, but approximately 30 minutes is a guideline.

When everyone has returned, take time to reflect together on their experiences, ideally seated around a campfire.

Silent Movement Games

Let's move on now to the matter of movement, or more precisely, the subject of sneaking. These games in particular demonstrate that learning can be fun and are helpful in bringing children's high energy down to appropriate levels for a nightwalk. Some of them are variations on games that you may well have played in childhood, but many are much older than that. These are exactly the sort of games I believe our indigenous ancestors would have played with their children as a way of practising essential skills and building awareness of predator and prey. Humans then were not the top of the food chain in many wilderness environments, and they had to be mindful of what might be stalking there. Learning the art of invisibility was an essential skill, as was learning how to move quietly towards animals and birds they wanted to catch and eat.

Here's a few of my favourites that work well for groups preparing to go out into the dark.

✦ ✦ ✦ ✦ ✦ ✦ ✦ ✦

FOX-WALKING

Teaching your companions how to fox-walk will pay dividends on any mission to get closer to wildlife, not least on a nightwalk when the target species have a highly developed sense of hearing. The simple idea of this exercise is to learn how to move silently through the undergrowth in a woods or forest. I advise spending the first bit of time directing the group's attention to the way they all walk naturally when they are not concentrating on being quiet, so that they can 'unlearn' this and instead copy how a fox might walk.

Equipment required:
None
Ages: 8 and up
Number of participants:
2–20

Ask the group to mill about, walking normally, and then encourage them to listen to the sounds their bodies and clothing make as they do so. Next, request the group continue to walk normally but this time to put their fingers in their ears, so they can 'hear' themselves 'on the inside'. This sounds strange I know, but it's very informative. Try it yourself ahead of time and you'll see how 'noisy' our walking is when experienced this way.

Tell the group to stop walking and gather around you. Now it's time to analyse 'normal' walking. Demonstrate how a person usually places their heel down first when walking along, followed by a roll of the foot towards the toes. Then demonstrate a fox-walk, which necessitates placing the toes down first, and then rolling the foot back towards the heel.

Get everyone in the group to try out fox-walking and experience the effect it has on their movement. They should notice right away that it necessitates slowing down from their usual walking pace. Next, ask the group to block their ears again and see what they hear and whether it's different.

Now add another instruction. Suggest to the group that to move as quietly as possible, they have to 'test' the ground underneath their feet with each step to check whether it's 'safe' to transfer their weight from one foot to the other. Most people are accustomed to 'falling' onto each foot when walking, transferring their weight unconsciously from foot to foot because there are no consequences to consider from doing so. Remind the group that the forest floor is littered with possible sound-producing natural debris like sticks and stones. Walking silently in the forest thus requires a softly-softly approach.

Demonstrate how to maintain weight on the standing foot, which enables us to explore the terrain under the toe of the forward foot and to consciously shift over our weight when it's safe to do so. Explain that in this way, we can quickly raise our foot if we suspect the transference of our weight will break a stick or leave us unbalanced on a stone.

Ask the group to practise consciously this method of weight transfer so that they retain precision control on each step. You can turn this into a little game by calling out 'freeze!' every so often, which will invariably cause some of your companions to practise balancing on one leg for a few seconds.

Here's one more challenge to present: stalking wildlife may well involve keeping your eyes up and focused on the creature you are stalking, rather than looking at your feet. (I've been caught out many times by looking down at the ground to secure my footing, only to realise I had lost sight of the deer or fox I was trailing when I looked up again.)

Ask the group to continue fox-walking but to now attempt it without looking at the ground. This presents a new challenge for our sense of balance, which instinctively harnesses our eyes to assist, but now requires our feet to 'see' the ground on which we are walking.

Notes and Variants

One last variation of fox-walking is to travel with your hands clasped either behind your back or in front of you. The point is to avoid moving your arms to help with balance. Any wild mammal or bird you might pursue will be very sensitive to movement. Keeping your hands joined together will not only reduce your visual profile, it will also prevent you from inadvertently drawing the creature's attention to your presence. It's not easy to fox-walk this way, so be patient as you practise.

It may not be appropriate to ask every group to achieve this level of quiet and focus, and you'll need to decide whether a night-time fox-walk is appropriate. Fox-walking outdoors at night may be too ambitious with a class of young schoolchildren, for example. It's still a fun exercise to practise, though, and introduces some basic principles to remember in terms of getting close to wildlife. It is also a skill they can 'take away' to practise on their own and teach others.

DEER STALK

Deer stalking is a good activity to follow a fox-walk. To start, ask everyone to stand in a big circle, spaced at least 'fingertip-to-fingertip' apart. If there's space, wider still. Position yourself in the middle of the circle.

Explain that you are a 'deer' and everyone else is a 'stalker', and that you are equipped with all of a deer's faculties of sensory perception. This means you have very acute senses of hearing and sight, and therefore they will

> **Equipment required:**
> None
> **Ages:** 8 and up
> **Number of participants:**
> 2–20

have to exercise extreme care as they try to approach you. Practising all they have learnt in their fox-walking, their goal is to move as close as they can without being 'caught'. In this case, being caught means the deer points at them because they have not been quiet or still enough. That, of course, is up to you as the deer to decide.

When someone is caught, there are a couple of options. They could sit down in place and be out of the game, or they could freeze for a certain time period before rejoining the game, which keeps them in play, but with a minor time penalty.

Notes
Before play begins, you may want to explain that just because the deer looks up from browsing, it does not necessarily get spooked and run away. This is true with real deer, too: to stay on an animal's trail sometimes requires being exposed in full view, but if you remain motionless, the sight of you won't necessarily unsettle the animal. This may happen in this game, too. If the deer is alerted to a stalker by sound or movement, that person should

keep perfectly still whilst being looked at, and possibly can reassure the deer they are not a threat.

Obviously, there will come a point where the stalkers get too close to the deer to remain unnoticed. At that point, you can announce game over and congratulate the group on their stalking skills. Usually the group will want to play again and you may try having them start farther away from you on the second round.

DEER STALK 2

This is a simple development on the Deer Stalk game that involves the group hiding themselves to start with whilst the deer's eyes are closed. Begin by explaining how to play this version.

Equipment required:
2 sticks, about 60–90 cm
   (24–36 inches) long, to
   use as 'legs'
Ages: 8 and up
Number of participants:
2–20

Rules

1. To start with, the deer closes their eyes and counts out loud to 20. As the deer counts, all the stalkers find a place to hide, such as behind a tree.
2. When the deer says, 'Game on,' the game begins.
3. The stalkers start to approach just as in the regular Deer Stalk game.
4. The deer now has its own agenda and can move in any direction to browse or graze. This makes it critical for the stalkers to keep their eye on the prey at all times.
5. As with regular Deer Stalk, the deer points out players who have not kept quiet or still enough, which results in a time penalty or simply being out for the rest of the game.

Notes

This game is much more fun if you embody and role-play a real deer, mimicking its movements and behaviour. This is where the sturdy sticks come in. Use them as your 'front legs', which will instantly turn you into a four-legged ungulate. As you browse through the terrain, any clumsy movements or sounds might spook you, and you can dash off in a brief sprint before turning around and looking back to see whether you have lost your pursuer. Improvise your actions in order to increase the difficulty for the stalkers to stay in the game. I advise not to eject players too early, though. Depending on the profile of the group, players may not have the capacity to sit out for a long time without distracting and disturbing the others. In total, the game can last between 5–10 minutes; if there is a good deal of focus, it may last even longer.

POKE THE GRIZZLY

Some legends are hard to believe, but this one persists. It suggests that the young men of some indigenous tribes of North America played this game to practise their stealth. This unlikely scenario involves stalking a bear, and the 'winner' would be the one who succeeded in getting so close to the bear they could surprise it by whacking it on the rump with a stick, and then (presumably) running for dear life.

> **Equipment required:**
> 1 rope, 5–10 metres (15–35 feet) long
> **Ages:** 6 and up
> **Number of participants:** 4–16

This game benefits from this narrative, whether it's true or not, as a context to set the scene. In fact, this is a twist on the game Grandmother's Footsteps, which is played by creeping up behind a 'grandmother' who has to keep turning around to try to catch sight of anyone moving. If you are frozen in place when she turns you stay in the game, which ends when someone manages to tap 'grandma' on the shoulder.

In this scenario, a 'grizzly bear' replaces 'grandmother', and the consequences for being the one to poke the bear is being chased by the disgruntled, growling and snarling bear.

Start by laying out the rope to make a start/finish line and ask players to line up along the rope. Explain the rules, then position yourself 10–20 metres (35–65 feet) away from the rope and turn your back to the players to start the game.

Rules

1. One player (you to start with) is the bear, who will stand with their back to the rest of the players. The goal of the game is to sneak up and poke the bear...
2. Once the bear signals the game to begin, players can cross the rope and try to sneak forward towards the bear.
3. Occasionally, the bear will turn around and point at anyone who was spotted moving (or is still moving). Those players must do the 'walk of shame' back to where they started, behind the rope, and join in again when play recommences. This keeps everyone in the game, but disadvantages those overeager types who haven't learnt to slow down.
4. If a player succeeds in reaching and poking the bear, that player must then run back and cross the finish line whilst the bear gives chase and tries to tag the player.
5. If the bear is successful in the chase, the victim becomes the new bear and the game resets.

Notes and Variants

When I lead this game, I often remind the players of the classic Aesop's fable *The Hare and the Tortoise*, which easily communicates the relevant learning point.

If you want to engender even more fun into this game, try a playful variation. For example, players could each carry a cup of water, which they then pour on the bear if they get close enough. Or, you could strew some items of clothing like shoes and hats across the play area. Players must pick up the items and put them on along the route. This both adds to the hilarity and makes the game more challenging.

SLOW RACE

Here's another game that emphasises the need to slow down to achieve quieter movement.

To begin, ask for an assistant to help you place a rope on the ground in a straight line – it needs to be long enough for the group to stand next to each other, shoulder to shoulder, in one line facing you. Ask everyone to stand so their toes are just touching the rope. Then ask the group to remain perfectly still, especially their feet, whilst you and your assistant lift the rope and set it down again a mere 2–3 metres (6–10 feet) away, so that everyone is equidistant from it. Thus, the players are now stood

> **Equipment required:**
> 1 rope long enough to serve as a finish line, about 5–10 metres (15–35 feet)
> **Ages:** 6 and up
> **Number of participants:** 6–20

on the starting line and they can see the finishing line. The rather ridiculous notion is then proposed to have a 'slow race'. The winner will be the *last* person across the finishing line, and the first person across is in fact going to end up as 'last' in the race.

Now, this is simple enough as a concept, and the players will immediately relish the idea. But next you must introduce rules, including the method of travel, so that everyone plays fair. This game can get a bit messy unless you clearly state what is allowed and what is considered 'cheating', but explain the rules with a sense of fun, rather than competition.

Rules

1. Once the 'starting gun' sounds, everyone must be seen to be continuously moving and always travelling forward.
2. The judge (you) will watch all players and point out anyone judged to have paused or gone backwards. Anyone thus caught must leave the race and becomes a judge.
3. The growing group of judges keeps monitoring the remaining 'athletes' to point out any transgressions.

4. As soon as a racer's toes touch the finish-line rope, they are out and they also join the judging team.

Invariably, the last three racers are egged on by the rest of the group, joining in with the Olympic role-play in good humour until the last person is left, at which point you can 'award' the bronze, silver and gold medals and move onto the next activity – unless everyone wants to play again, which, if it's a group of kids, they inevitably will!

RING THE BELL

Variations on this game have been played all over the world for thousands of years, partly as an instructional aid to practise the important business of learning to move quietly, and partly because it's thrilling. It's no surprise that in Britain alone it goes by different names in different regions of the country, including Keeper of the Keys and Dragon's Treasure.

Equipment required:
Sit mats
Bell (or other 'treasure')
Blindfold
Torch (if dark)
Ages: 6 and up
Number of participants:
8–25

The game is played by a circle of people around a blindfolded 'keeper' in the middle, who either sits or stands. A bell (or keys, or whistle, etc.) is placed between the keeper's toes or knees. The object of the game is for one 'hunter' to sneak up to the keeper and ring the bell before being detected. As the leader, your role in this game is to facilitate rather than to actively take part. Once everyone has formed a circle, explain the rules below, then wait until everyone is quiet and settled to begin the game.

Rules

1. The facilitator chooses one player to be the first keeper who goes to the middle of the circle and is blindfolded.

2. Next, the facilitator chooses one player to be the first hunter.

3. When the game begins, the keeper must listen for the hunter moving and should point precisely in the direction of any sounds they hear. The facilitator will then shout 'freeze' if the keeper has successfully pointed at a hunter or 'no' if not. The keeper then points again in the direction of any sounds.

4. The hunter begins to move, carefully and quietly, towards the keeper.

5. The keeper listens for any sound of approach. When they hear someone, they point in that direction to pinpoint the hunter.

6. If the facilitator can see that the keeper has pointed accurately towards the hunter, the facilitator shouts 'freeze' and also points at the perpetrator. That hunter must now remain frozen in place, no longer part of the action. If the keeper was wrong, the hunter can continue to creep forward.

7. As the game progresses, the facilitator designates more hunters, so that usually a few are making the attempt at the same time.

8. Once a hunter succeeds in ringing the bell, they become the new keeper.

Notes and Variants

Before the game starts, emphasise that everyone must keep quiet, even when it's not their turn to hunt. This avoids confusing the keeper. For this reason, it's often better to ask the players to sit on mats in a circle and remain sitting until their turn starts, although this represents more of a challenge in beginning the stalking.

Use your discretion about the timing of adding additional hunters to the game. It's a question of not overwhelming the keeper with too many hunters at once, and sustaining everyone's interest by keeping them involved and active.

If you are playing this game with children younger than eight, you'll need to spell out the importance of slow-motion movement, especially when getting close to the keeper. Otherwise, the children are likely to rush forward, diving on top of the bell in their enthusiasm to win, leaving the keeper no time to point. Explain that there is no skill in this approach, and that the objective is to learn to move slowly and keep calm, just like you would have to in order to stay on the trail of a real animal.

The terrain underfoot is a critical factor, which will determine how easy or difficult the game will be. Consider in advance the profile of your group, especially how old they are. You could start off in an easier patch of ground such as in long grass, and then progress onto something more challenging like the forest floor. If you think a group is up to the challenge, choose a site where there are obstacles to negotiate like bushes, boulders or brambles.

To add an extra dimension to the game, you can bury the bell under sticks or leaf litter. This demands even more concentration from the hunter who has arrived at the keeper's feet and must then work slowly and carefully to get to the bell.

Another variation on this game is to allow it to continue after the first hunter succeeds. In this case, instruct the hunters to only touch the 'treasure' rather than taking it. Then they must return to the edge of the circle, if possible without being caught. This requires even greater self-control if the treasure is an edible treat like a tempting bowl of raspberries or marshmallows.

A cheeky variation, which kids (and even adults) will love is to arm the keeper with one of those long, foam swimming aids called noodles to use in place of pointing at hunters. Charge the group with the task of either ringing the bell or, alternatively, tagging the keeper without getting walloped by the noodle. Players are either required to return to the circle to try again if hit by the noodle or instead to sit down and be out of the game.

TOLLKEEPER

The gist of this sneaking game is to quietly bypass the 'tollkeeper' who will try to catch out 'travellers' in the light of their torch. You can play this game in an open area or somewhere along a forest trail.

Designate a person to be the tollkeeper who will sit, blindfolded. Explain that their task will be to guard the 'passage' or 'bridge' or 'tunnel', whichever scenario you prefer. Equip the tollkeeper with a torch to shine at anyone they hear passing by. Caution them not to sweep the torch back and forth, but rather to aim directly at specific sounds of movement nearby.

Lay out two short ropes to mark the edges of the 'home ground' or 'safety zone' at a distance of about 8–10 metres (27–35 feet) to either side of the tollkeeper. Lay the long rope as a 'hand-rail' for the stalkers to follow, to ensure they stay in range of the tollkeeper.

Divide the players into two groups of travellers and set up one group to wait in each safety zone. (This is to avoid long queues, which can be a frustration for impatient children.)

The object of the game is for a traveller to creep past the tollkeeper without being tagged by the light before they cross over the rope on the far side and into that safety zone.

Equipment required:
Sit mat
Torch
Blindfold
2 short ropes, 1–2 metres (4–7 feet) long
1 long rope, 8–10 metres (27–35 feet) long
Water pistol or plant sprayer (optional)
Ages: 6 and up
Number of participants: 8–20

If a traveller is hit by the tollkeeper's light as they try to sneak past, they freeze on the spot. Change roles once a few hunters have been frozen or, if the group is small, after everyone has had a chance to try sneaking past.

Notes and Variants

The trail can also be defined by suspending a long rope between two trees so that it serves as a literal handrail for the travellers to follow using their hands, with the tollkeeper positioned at the middle point of the rope and about 2 metres (7 feet) away from the rope. If using this rope trail method, you can move the rope closer in to the tollkeeper each time, to make it more challenging.

If you are playing this game during the day, the tollkeeper can use a water pistol or plant sprayer rather than a torch to 'tag' players as they pass by. You can even use the water pistol in conjunction with the torch at night, if your group is up for it. The water element does make the game a lot more fun!

HUNTERS

This edgy-but-fun game of stealth quickly teaches the players of the need for slow, careful movement and a much deeper listening.

Inside a defined area – a rope circle or the group standing or sitting in a circle – select two members of the group to play in the 'arena' and blindfold them. The object of the game is for each player to 'hunt' their opponent, endeavouring to touch them between the shoulder blades to take them out of the game. Everyone else has to remain silent, so as not to interfere whilst the hunters listen as closely as possible to figure out where the other one is. Those at the edge of the circle can help out as needed by gently tapping the hunters on the shoulder if they are venturing too close to the circle's perimeter.

Equipment required:
2 blindfolds
Long rope (optional)
Ages: 10 and up
Number of participants:
6–12

Each time a hunter is tagged out, the leader designates a new hunter to enter the area. Adding in additional players heightens the tension (and entertainment!), creating a more complex dynamic.

PREDATOR AND PREY

This game is a way to introduce the predator–prey relationship, to mimic the natural world's dance of survival, as well as to practise silent movement and sensory awareness.

Before diving into the game's setup and rules, you might ask the group to think of examples from nature of predators and their prey, and then specifically from the habitat you are in. Explain that this game puts the players into the roles of predator and prey. Each role is different, but both are dependent on keen abilities to hear, smell, see and move silently.

The object of the game is for the 'predator' to locate and try to capture the 'prey' by tapping the prey between the shoulder blades.

Start by defining a circular playing field. You can use a rope to mark the edge of the circle, or simply ask the players to stand or sit in a circle.

Ask for two volunteers to begin. Have them step into the circle. Designate one player as the predator and the other as the prey. Explain that all the predator has to do is locate the prey

Equipment required:
Blindfolds
Bells
Long rope (optional)
Ages: 8 and up
Number of participants:
8–20

and try to capture them. All the prey has to do is evade capture. The overall guidelines for the Hunters game also apply here.

Notes and Variants

As with other stalking games, the advantage is very much with the prey, because movement causes sound. Prey animals usually have sensitive hearing or a keen sense of smell. To imitate the advantage that prey has over predator, the predator can be fitted out with a blindfold. Or bells can be strapped on the predator's ankle, which will tinkle whenever the predator moves.

Establishing certain ground rules will ensure the success of the game. Restrict the players to moving in slow motion or, at the most, at walking pace. Suggest that the players mimic the kind of movement of the prey–predator examples discussed.

If the predator is not succeeding and you sense the game is starting to drag, then reduce the size of the circle to make a smaller hunting ground.

Watching the fascinating movement sequence can be as much fun for the observers as the two players in the circle. There is a steep learning curve here for everyone as they work out strategies for more success as the predator or the prey.

After a few games, try introducing an extra dimension, again to mimic the natural world's processes. Ask the group whether they can name a food chain of predators and prey in which there are more than two protagonists. Often, the examples given will be from faraway places, like lion–jackal–meercat. Focus the players' attention on creatures who live in your local area. In a forest habitat, examples might be badger–hedgehog–slug, owl–shrew–beetle, buzzard–bat–mosquito or heron–frog–fly.

For the ultimate game of predator–prey, introduce a third player: the super-predator. The rules of this engagement will be that the predator must hunt the prey, whilst also watching out to avoid being captured by the super-predator. Try to find two sets of bells that ring in different tones to help the prey distinguish the predator from the super-predator.

LANTERN STALK

For those afraid of the dark, this game is one of the best to help allay fears and build confidence. This is a team game in which one team tries to quietly stalk up through the shadows cast by a lantern across an open area of woodland whilst the other team tries to spot and capture them. The object of the game is for the stalkers to make as much progress as they can towards the lantern, from positions that are initially quite far away; for the other team, the object is to accurately detect and capture as many stalkers as they can. It's important to choose an area for playing that is open enough so as not to restrict movement, but not devoid of features to hide behind.

Equipment required:
Gas lantern (or some other
    device with equivalent
    light intensity)
1 rope, 12–15 metres
    (40–50 feet) long
Ages: 8 and up
Number of participants:
8–30

Place the unlit lantern at the centre of the playing area, lay out the rope in a circle about 3–4 metres (10–15 feet) in diameter around the lantern and ask the players to gather around. Explain the rules of the game and then divide the group into two or three teams.

Rules

1. Group 1 are the lantern-keepers. They gather around the lantern and close their eyes. The lantern is then lit, but Group 1 players keep their eyes closed.

2. State how long the game will last overall (15 minutes can be a good length for the first round of play). At your signal, Group 2 players head away from the lantern to take shelter in the shadows. Allow them about 2 minutes to 'dissolve' into the darkness. During this time, Group 1 can quietly discuss their strategy for capturing the most 'prisoners'.

3. When the 2 minutes is up, and when (hopefully) none of the stalkers can be seen or heard, shout, 'Game on!' The lantern keepers then turn outward, putting their backs to the light, and open their eyes. The lantern-keepers can move about, but they must stay within the rope circle around the lantern.

4. The lantern-keepers can take 'shots' to capture prisoners by pointing out to the facilitator (you) any stalker they think they have detected, showing the location as precisely as they can. You then head off in that direction, and if you find someone roughly in that area, you tap them on the shoulder and escort them to a predetermined 'prison' area, where they must sit quietly to wait out the rest of the game.

5. If a lantern-keeper makes an inaccurate shot and you find no stalker there, it goes down as a 'miss.' There is a limited allowance of misses (three to five), after which the lantern-keepers have no shots left. This usually has the required effect of reducing the number of wild, speculative shots, with you endlessly trammelling up and down as the gofer. … A tiresome occupation!

6. The game ends when you give the signal. I like to end the action by shouting, 'Game over! Show yourselves!' At that point, those still uncaptured will dramatically reveal themselves, with glee, from their hiding place, popping out from behind a fallen tree or standing up in the middle of a bush or wherever they have got to.

The teams then switch roles and the game is played again. You can keep a tally of the prisoners caught so that by the end of the second round there is a winner, but this element of competition is rarely required, the game having enough edge and excitement to be enjoyable even without keeping score.

Notes and Variants

When you explain the rules, it's worth clarifying that the task for the stalkers is to make some progress, rather than simply sitting behind a tree for the duration. That's because whilst sitting still might help them build a relationship with the dark, it does not meet the practising silent movement criteria.

A detail to emphasise is that success is measured in terms of progress made. Whilst being undetected by simply hiding behind a big tree is enough to stay in the game, there is less skill and therefore satisfaction involved than if you start off further away and make progress via shadow and stealth to get closer to the lantern. With larger numbers, you can divide the group into three or four teams. Each team takes turns to defend the lantern whilst everyone else stalks in as one competing body.

One exciting development of the game is to allow two of the lantern-keepers to 'enter the night arena', leaving the restriction of the rope circle to actively search for stalkers, finding them in their hiding places and sending them to the prison area.

Inevitably, all the lantern-keepers will want a turn being mobile, so you can call in the first pair after a few minutes and send out the next.

With this added challenge for the stalkers, the big reveal at the end is even more triumphant for those who survived the hunt, an exhilarating achievement!

For a bit of extra fun, quietly hand the two lantern-keepers a water pistol or Nerf gun as they head out into the darkness!

PREDATOR

Similar to Lantern Stalk, but even more fun. However, it's not a game for the faint of heart. Predator is best with a group of teens or adults, or children who are accompanied by adults. The object of the game is for teams of players to cross the arena without being intercepted and killed by a 'predator' who lies in wait.

To prepare for this game, find a reasonably open area in the woods, approximately 75–100 metres (85–110 yards) across. Hang two glow sticks from low branches, one at either end of your designated arena. Different coloured lights help to distinguish the two areas. Adjust the length of the arena according to the terrain and how dark it is. At a halfway point, but to one side, identify a waiting area where you can hang or place a lantern.

Divide the group into two teams and also designate someone to be the 'predator'. Light the lantern in the waiting area and then explain the rules.

Equipment required:
2 glow sticks of different
  colours
Water pistol or plant sprayer
Candle lantern or differently
  coloured glow stick for
  the 'prison'
Sit mats
Ages: 8 and up
Number of participants:
10-30

Rules

1. Before play begins, each team gathers at either end of the playing area under a glow stick and discusses tactics for a few minutes.
2. When the start signal is given, each team must then attempt to cross the arena and gather under the glow stick at the other end. The more individuals from a team that reach their destination, the more points they will gain.
3. The predator, who is armed with the plant sprayer or water pistol, lurks in the shadows with the sole ambition of squirting anyone trying to sneak past them!
4. Any players who are hit by a stream of water are out of the action. They must head quietly down to the spot where the lantern has been lit, to sit with others and reflect upon the error of their noisy ways.
5. Play lasts about 15 minutes, at which time you give the signal – a shout of 'Game over!' or blowing a whistle, etc. Gather everyone down at the lantern area to tot up the numbers from each team that safely reached the other side.

Notes and Variants

Encourage some strategic thinking at the outset and give various options as to how players might decide to travel. For example, they can stay together if nervous. Contrast that strategy with the effectiveness of operating alone.

It adds a wonderful drama if the predator's victims 'die' noisily and dramatically – there's nothing quite like a terrifying scream in the forest at night to unsettle the nerves. A long, drawn out, overacted 'death' is sure to prompt some stifled giggles in the dark...

Those with an aversion to playing with gun-like toys could use a plant sprayer as an alternative to water pistols. Find one that has a good range, but can still be easily carried.

When I lead this game with a mixed-age group, I usually take the role of predator to start, or offer it to another adult in order to model the skills required: moving quietly and unobtrusively to surprise the players. The game is better when a few 'kills' take place relatively quickly during the first round of play; it sets a benchmark for subsequent predators to try to meet.

Depending on the size of the group, you can designate more than one predator to increase the chances that some players will be hit as they traverse the playing area. And if the groups you're leading are incentivised by friendly competition, the scores can accumulate over successive games until you have a champion team.

FIRE STALK

This is a lovely, collaborative activity if you have the right setting and, of course, permission to build a blazing campfire. It's quite similar to the Lantern Stalk game, with the main difference being that you don't divide the group into teams.

The best set-up is to walk your group around the circumference of the campfire at dusk and to drop them off, well-spaced apart, for a short sit-spot. Then, their task will be, on a given signal – like a drumbeat or a conch – to stalk in and get as close to the fire as possible, under cover of the darkness, without being seen by those who are 'guarding' the fire.

You can ask a few players to serve as 'guards' and stay near the fire, or the guard can just be yourself to start with. The way this activity develops and keeps everyone engaged is to recruit more guards whenever someone is spotted. Of course, the name of the game is to remain undetected; easily achieved if you don't risk coming close and the simple matter of dwelling in the dark is a potent experience for those unaccustomed to it. The holy grail, however, is to sneak in as close as possible and when the signal for the game to end is given, you spring out with a triumphant shout.

> **Equipment required:**
> Campfire
> Water pistols, plant sprayers
> or Nerf guns (optional)
> **Ages:** 8 and up
> **Number of participants:**
> 10–30

Notes and Variants

How far away from the fire you travel during the initial set-up will depend on the age profile and capacity of the group, and the terrain you are in. Scope this out in advance and in daylight to avoid any literal and figurative pitfalls. A dense and impenetrable bramble patch or even a thicket of holly, for example, can be an intense physical challenge for a robust adult group but a trauma zone for youngsters. Don't underestimate the darkness for its ability to ramp up the threat level. What seems easy to you by day can present problems at night. In short, you need to think carefully what sort of experience you are offering in this – either a difficult and visceral one, or a more subtle and nuanced acquaintance with the dark. Mostly, I design the latter kind of experience, as creeping about in the dark is in itself enough of an adventure.

You can always invite the group to start the activity by leaving the fireside to find their own route out into the darkness beyond, and therefore they can self-guide themselves to where their edge might be; some might start further away, some closer in. The important thing to emphasise is the specific task to achieve some distance between where they start and where they finish.

If you wish, you can arm all the stalkers with water pistols or plant sprayers or Nerf guns and their endgame is to squirt or shoot a guard whilst remaining undetected.

DRUM STALK

Similar to Fire Stalk, this activity has the same geometry with a slightly different emphasis: the group will use their ears to attune themselves to the landscape. Depending on the size of the group, you may need the help of several assistants for this activity. Take note, it can be played in both day and night; both require a blindfold to be worn.

Equipment required:
Drum
Sit mats
Blindfolds
Torches for the helpers (if
  playing at night)
Ages: 11 and up
Number of participants:
6–16

Start by walking everyone in a wide circle around a fixed point, which is wherever the drumbeat will be played from. Again, the size of the circle area will be defined by the size of the group and the capacity of the participants. The terrain will also dictate the distance it is possible to travel at night and/or blindfolded, so you need to adapt it accordingly. For example, a heavily wooded area will necessitate a smaller circle than an open area.

Assess how long it will take someone who is blindfolded to find their way into the centre. I would suggest about 15–20 minutes is challenging enough, although for some more mature groups who might relish this adventure, you could stretch this 30 or even 40 minutes.

As the group makes the circuit, you and your assistants seat each person individually and blindfold them. (Take note, a blindfold is imperative whether playing this game by day or night, because it preserves the sense of 'blindness' that the activity depends upon.)

When all are seated, the drum will begin to play. Beginning when they hear the first single beat of the drum, their task is to find their way to the drum.

Every so often, another drumbeat will sound to orientate them in which direction to travel. The time between the drumbeats can be as long as a minute.

On arrival to the central point, each participant is met by assistants who will guide them silently to a seat and instruct them to keep their blindfold on and remain silent. When everyone is 'home', the blindfolds can be removed.

Some reflection should then take place, ideally in pairs to begin with and then a whole group reflection process on what the experience was like.

Notes and Variants

Once everyone has made the trek and is seated around the drummer, I sometimes tell a story before they remove their blindfolds. This can be very powerful as the atmosphere may be charged with emotion, with the sense of having been through something significant. If you decide to try this, choose a story that strikes the right tone and make it relatively short – no more than 8 minutes long. To avoid an unnecessarily exhaustive search for traditional narratives, how about you undertake to write one yourself? Then you can make it fit for purpose.

Ask your assistants to stay alert and rove around during the drum stalk to keep everyone from going off-piste. Coach the assistants in advance that their role is to quietly support the participants' progress, but with as little intervention as possible. There might be occasions where someone needs help to get out of an entanglement, but the overall rule is to preserve the illusion that participants are 'on their own'.

Don't underestimate how impactful this experience can be for some people. They may well need some quiet time following it. Check in with anyone who is especially quiet or appears caught in the grip of emotion.

One last note for this activity more than any other: be sure to experience it yourself first, so you know exactly what sort of experience you are putting others through.

GHOST IN THE GRAVEYARD

One of those simple hiding/chasing games that is easy to play in the dark and will have children enjoying themselves so much that they won't remember their fear of the dark.

Equipment required:
Torches
Ages: 7 and up
Number of participants:
4–18

The campfire can serve as a base, or alternatively, you could place a candle lantern in open ground. The players assemble at the base and one or two 'ghosts' are chosen to go off and hide. Meanwhile, with their eyes shut, the ghost-hunters count out loud to twenty and then shout 'ghost-hunters!'. At this point, they turn on their torches and begin to scour the surrounding area. When someone discovers a 'ghost', they shout 'ghost in the graveyard!' and everyone races to get back to the base area before the ghost(s) can tag them. Anyone who is caught is, needless to say, consigned to be the 'ghost' for the next game.

A ratio of one 'ghost' to eight 'ghost-hunters' works well. With a larger number of players, more 'ghosts' can be chosen.

CHAPTER 4

Discovering Nocturnal Creatures

One should pay attention to even the smallest crawling creature,
for these too may have a valuable lesson to teach us.

BLACK ELK

L ight is a factor that determines much of the behaviour and characteristics of animals, and evolution has gone to extraordinary
lengths to ensure that adaptations to conditions of bright or dim
light are effective in prolonging the existence of a species. For example, in
the mysterious inky-black ocean depths where even angels fear to tread,
there are fish whose prey is so scarce they have developed a rod-like structure with an illuminated 'lantern' at the end that projects from their heads
and attracts the small prey fish to their jaws.

Our nocturnal creatures in Britain are no less well adapted to operating
at night even if they don't hunt by swinging a torch to catch their prey. I
think they are no less fascinating, and the more you find out about them
the more interesting they become. (A bit like people, really.)

We are blessed these days with an exotic array of wildlife documentaries
that depict rare, endangered or downright mystifying creatures from all
over the world. It's therefore easy to assume that our own back garden of
animals in Britain could never compare with, say, a pride of lions or a great
white shark.

In my experience, introducing people to the 'secret commonwealth' of
nocturnal nature in Britain, however, it turns out that nothing could be

further than the truth. The thrill of seeing real, wild animals, especially in the rarefied conditions of the night, is consistently a peak experience. Presumably, that's because our excursions into the dark are so uncommon. We usually spend our evenings indoors, and even when we go outside it's for a late-evening dog walk under the streetlights, not a ramble through wild nature. Thus the 'wow' factor when a wild creature shows up. I've heard it hundreds of times and it's one of my favourite natural sounds of all, the exclamations of people thrilled by Britain's wildlife.

Nocturnal nature can put on quite a show for the determined and discerning naturalist, and if you know what and where to look and listen for, it can offer a feast of opportunities to get close to our wildlife, which can be more elusive by day.

The activities in this chapter will help persuade children, teens and adults accustomed to the ordinary comforts of the indoors to step out over the day/night threshold and go in search of wildlife. I explain how you can maximise your wildlife encounters for yourself and others, with just a few simple techniques. Although it's beyond the scope of this book to introduce all of the creatures of the night fully and completely, I have paired up the activity descriptions with some curious facts and intriguing stories of the wildlife champions of the night and the ones you are most likely to encounter on a nightwalk in field or woodland.

NOSES

This guessing game has a fun distinguishing feature: it invites players to place a finger on their nose when they think they know the answer. It's a great game to create some intrigue – and to stealthily impart some good old natural history – before playing an animal-specific game like Bat and Moth or undertaking an activity like bat detecting.

The object of the game is to figure out the identity of a mystery creature by listening to the leader (you) reveal a series of clues. These clues are general at first – 'it's a mammal' and 'it hibernates'. Then they slowly become more and more specific to build a picture of a particular animal – 'it flies' and 'it's an insectivore'. And by clue ten or twelve you are practically giving

away the answer – 'it hangs upside down!' The goal is to ensure
that everyone's noses are covered
by the last clue, and then all can
share in the fun of shouting out
the animal's identity.

Equipment required:
None
Ages: 6 and up
Number of participants:
4 or more

Notes and Variants

You can prepare clues for any animal you want to introduce on a nightwalk.
Just follow the pattern of starting with general clues that gradually become
more obvious. Eight to twelve clues should suffice.

About Small Mammals

Let's hear it for these little champions! Small mammals are a prolific and
industrious contingent found in diverse habitats the world over. Wherever
they go, the hunters will follow – let's not forget that they are what sustain
the populations of their predators. This makes them a key piece in the
jigsaw puzzle of ecology.

It's not hard to spot small mammals in their environment, assuming you
can adhere to the general rules of stillness and focus. In fact, they will often
be the surprise and delight during a sit-spot or badger watch, scuttling
about at your feet or squeaking in the undergrowth. One of my teachers
once set me the lovely exercise of lying on the ground and plunging my
head into a hedge for two hours to observe the small mammal scene. A
rewarding endeavour if you have the patience.

Shrews

Shrews are insectivores and so are characterised by their busy, energetic
and nervous disposition. The UK boasts five species of shrew, with only
three likely to be encountered on the mainland, the other two species are
limited to the Scilly and Channel islands. The **common shrew** generally
outnumbers the tiny **pygmy shrew** by about five to one, but the reverse
is true in sand dune and upland habitats. The common shrew likes to eat
earthworms, which it finds on its hunting missions through its burrows.
The pygmy shrew eschews earthworms, foraging in the leaf litter for insects.

Shrews are the type of corpse we most often come across on the trail, but that's not because they are hunted more than mice or voles. More likely it's because the predator, usually a cat, has decided against eating it due to some distasteful scent glands on its flanks.

The larger and darker coloured **water shrew** hunts in and around streams for aquatic invertebrates and even small fish and frogs. Small hairs on its feet and tail help it manoeuvre in the water.

Voles

There's one species of vole in Britain that lives in and around water. This vole is the character in Kenneth Grahame's *The Wind in the Willows*, confusingly named Ratty, and is larger and heavier-bodied than its cousins. This characterisation is indicative of a wider confusion around the **water vole**, which is often referred to as a 'water rat', an unwelcome association with its unpopular, non-native and distant cousins that have colonised Britain, the brown rat and the black rat.

Look for evidence of water voles in the form of closely cropped vegetation near the openings of their riverbank burrows, which can be above or below water level. These endearing creatures make a gentle plopping sound as they drop into the water, usually to escape your approach. It's estimated that 90 per cent of our populations have succumbed to diverse pressures on our waterways, including the successfully adapted mink, released from fur farms a few decades ago.

In a strange twist of irony the **common vole** is not common at all. Absent entirely from the mainland, it is an island dweller, with Guernsey a stronghold.

Field voles and **bank voles** are the other main players in the vole team, and these are abundant throughout Britain, with the field vole being the most common.

These voles look quite similar, but the tail of the field vole is relatively shorter and its fur tends towards grey, as opposed to the slightly more reddish colouring of the bank vole. But they prefer different habitats, with the latter in hedge banks, and the former in open fields and meadows. If you spot some vole droppings, note the colour: greenish likely indicates the product of the grass-eating field vole; brownish, the bank vole.

Field studies of voles suggest that they are safer on rainy nights because the noise from rain on leaf litter shields their presence from owls. The rain

Safe Trapping

Trapping mice and voles in a live trap seems like fun and affords us the opportunity for close observation, but also causes them stress. An alternative is to use a footprint tube to capture the trails these small mammals leave behind. These can either be round plastic pipes or triangular cardboard tunnels, approximately 6–12 cm (3–6 inches) in diameter and perhaps 30 cm (12 inches) in length. You can obtain these from DIY stores or natural history retailers, or easily make one out of cardboard. An empty Tetra Pak carton can also be used. To make a pair of ink pads, stick a piece of greaseproof paper on both ends of the floor of your tunnel. Paint the pieces with a solution made of charcoal (or non-toxic paint) and vegetable oil. Bait the middle with something like peanut butter to tempt the little critters inside and leave it somewhere you think small mammals are active. Check regularly to see if you've 'caught' anything and to see what print calligraphy they leave behind.

This whole operation can be scaled up to capture the footprints of larger mammals like weasels and stoats.

also washes away scent trails that smell-focused predators rely on. So then, if you want to go vole hunting, try it on a night of light rain.

Mice

Perhaps the easiest of all British mammals to spot are the mice. In particular is the ubiquitous **house mouse**, the one non-native of our four species. Hailing originally from Asia, it has now settled successfully into British life and is never far away from habitation.

If the house mouse is the character Town Mouse from the children's book, then the burrowing **wood mouse** could be Country Mouse and is one of our most common mammals. Supremely adaptable in terms of diet and habitat, this mouse can in fact be found everywhere, and its predilection for nocturnal activity is given away by larger ears and more prominent eyes than the house mouse. Its lighter reddish-brown colouring, with a creamy-white chest and belly, makes it a more attractive beast than the house mouse – in my eyes anyway.

More confusing to tell apart, however, is the larger **yellow-necked field mouse**, which is, as its name suggests, distinguished from the other species by a clearer yellowish collar under its chin, but this is hard to spot. Then there is the tiny **harvest mouse**, which makes its home in cornfields and reed beds. Its cleverly crafted tell-tale nest hangs well above ground level in whatever tall vegetation will suit. This enables it to exploit a different niche whilst being safe from the threat of flooding. Should you get up close and personal, its smaller ears, blunt nose and prehensile tail also help to distinguish it from the wood mouse.

Last and not least, the **dormouse** deserves a mention because it is just the cutest thing! The capacity of dormice for long hibernations is legendary. They are active between May and October, but stay hidden in the thick canopy of coppiced woods. This result of human endeavour has been beneficial for the dormouse who prefers to move about 'upstairs' where the canopy has grown thick from the coppicing. A diet of nuts, seeds and berries suffices for this diminutive little charmer. Perfectly formed circular holes in hazelnut carcasses will probably be the only sign you'll find that dormice are present.

OWLS AND VOLES

In this game of predator–prey, the 'owls' hunt the 'voles' (and other small mammals) in and around some 'trees' in an attempt to catch a meal. In advance, recruit a few grown-ups to be the owls. Then ask your group to gather in a circle. Posing a series of questions can begin to arouse interest in the species involved in this game. What do tawny owls eat? How do they find their way in the dark? How can the small mammals protect themselves from predators at night?

Next, set the scene of the forest at night. Ask who would like to be the trees? Tell those volunteers to step into the circle and ask them to space themselves apart and 'make like trees'! Once those players are in position with arms akimbo as statuesque tree sculptures, ask the rest of the group to become voles and mice and shrews that squeak and scuttle about, foraging amongst the trees. Allow the small mammals a little rehearsal time before introducing the predators.

Now it's time to cue the owls into action, ideally with an owl hoot. When the signal hoot is given, the small mammals freeze as the owls open their wings (arms) out wide and begin to swoop between the trees looking for prey. They will capture any small mammal that they see moving, even blinking, dragging them out of the forest arena to join the circle. After a few sequences like this, change the cast of characters around so everyone takes turns in all three roles.

The game ends with the invitation: 'Now, let's go on a real owl hunt!'

> **Equipment required:**
> Owl call – a whistle or a recording
> **Ages:** 6 and up
> **Number of participants:** 8–25

About Owls

Collective noun: a parliament

You just gotta love owls! One of nocturnal nature's ambassadors and so familiar to almost all human cultures. Owls are a kind of caricature of the night, even though not all owl species are strictly nocturnal. There are, in fact, relatively few nocturnal birds and you might wonder why this is so. The answer is that birds are more visual creatures, and have not evolved the sensory criteria to navigate and feed at night and avoid predators. With their hollow bones, a reduced vertebra (no tail bone) and an absence of teeth, birds function best during the day, with very few exceptions.

Britain now plays host to seven species of owl, although the **snowy owl** hardly counts as it's an exceptionally rare visitor to the islands north of Scotland. Another unusual sighting is the **eagle owl**, which has recently bred here in Britain since escaping from captivity. Whilst the RSPB declare otherwise, the World Owl Trust cites evidence of these impressive owls once being native to Britain.

Tawny owls and **barn owls** are the most common. Of the others, the **little owl**, a diminutive version of the tawny owl, was introduced in the nineteenth century and has found its ecological niche in mixed habitats of copses and fields where it can hunt large insects without competing with other birds of prey. The **short-eared** and **long-eared** owls aren't widespread, so are less familiar, generally preferring the north to the south of Britain. Try looking for the former in the heath and moorland habitats where its more pointed wings can distinguish its flight. The latter is more associated with conifer woods and has the more familiar rounded wings of its tawny competitor. Both have 'ears' that are not ears at all, but tufts of feathers on their heads that play a role in expressing behaviours and moods. Both are after small mammals as prey, with field voles at the top of their shopping list.

Tawny Owls

Old country names: hill hooter, ferny hoolet, wood owl, wink-a-puss

For some creatures, the darkest nights provide optimum hunting conditions. The tawny owl is a consistent consumer throughout the year – the greater length of winter nights means more hunting hours, and so for these creatures there is a profit to be made at this supposedly less fruitful time of year.

The tawny owl is the commonest species in Britain, though somehow they remain elusive and beyond most people's gaze.

Owls stay silent when they hunt, and although their eyesight is good they rely on hearing to guide most of their navigation and hunting. Their ears are spaced to enable them to pinpoint prey by the differential in the time it takes for sound to reach each ear. Their satellite disc-like concave eye 'sockets' also funnel sound wave vibrations into their hearing system, literally directing them towards their ears. Soft feathers muffle any sound of flight and so their prey don't hear them approach. They have been recorded hunting on the wing, as well as from a perch and sometimes this extends to snatching unsuspecting birds from poorly located nests.

Tawny owls can't afford to be fussy eaters because nights are not always quiet. In windy or wet conditions where competing sounds muffle the movements of prey, tawny owls will scratch around on the ground for beetles or worms. Otherwise, their staple is small mammals like voles, shrews and mice. Frogs, lizards, birds and bats can also be prey items, and they have even been suspected of poaching fish as they surface from garden ponds.

> *Owl considers himself the most informed creature in*
> *the Wood.*
> **A.A. MILNE**

Hunting grounds range from 12 to 25 hectares (30 to 60 acres) on average in the UK, but size varies widely according to food supply. For example, an owl in Norway was found to be operating in a fairly prey-deficient 102 hectares (250 acres).

They enjoy deciduous and mixed woodland habitats and are spread fairly widely across the UK. However, tawny owls seem to be reluctant to cross any large water body which helps explain their absence from Britain's islands, including Ireland.

The average life span of a tawny owl is only 4 years and they mature quickly in order to breed at the end of their first year. The oldest recorded in the UK was a ringing recovery and was 23 years and 6 months – that's old for a bird. Tawny owls have a rather sweet courtship routine. The male owl woos his lover with a little swaying from side to side, then an up and down movement followed by raising first one wing, then the other. And just to really knock her off her perch, he might grunt a little, move his talon back and forth along the branch or indulge himself in a few wing-claps in chasing her about. Oh, what a charmer! All she has to do to show her approval is puff out and shiver her feathers. It's almost a true love story, but not quite. Tawny owls are generally monogamous, but polygamy prevails in some males.

March and April are the egg-laying months, but beware getting too close to the nest in this season as many have testified to being attacked by protective parent birds.

On a more sombre note, this bird has been placed on the amber list (of Birds of Conservation Concern) due to a puzzling slow decline in population in the UK.

There is a rich and diverse folklore around owls. Here in Britain we tend to characterise them as wise but conversely in many parts of the world they were an ill-omen. For example, in North America they were seen as bad news by many Native American nations, with parents even telling their children to behave 'lest the owls get them'. The French divide owls into 'eared' and 'earless'; the ones with 'ears' are wise and the ones without are unlucky.

Barn Owls

Old country names: Billy wix, pudge owl

There are few more arresting sights in the British countryside than watching the spectral grace of the barn owl hunting over a meadow at dusk. It's always a sublime moment as it weaves back and forth looking for small mammals that are stuffed throughout the species-rich grasslands.

Adding to its ghostly character is its ghoulish vocalisation, which can be unnerving indeed. Like most owls, it does not hoot at all, but issues forth a hoarse whispery screech that is undeniably creepy.

Sadly, populations of barn owls have diminished because of the introduction of intensive farm practices that have removed most of our wildlife-rich meadows. On a more positive note, the decline has at least been halted thanks to the wonderful conservation efforts made by a conglomerate of organisations, not least the Barn Owl Trust. And the barn owl has some wider success than its travails in blighted Britain, as it can be found on other continents.

Barn owls are so-called because they will adapt their nesting habits to make use of old barns. But it's also because they favour open country and so the agricultural landscape is where they can hunt for voles and mice along ditches and verges. Unlike the tawny owl, which can adapt its diet to include worms and beetles, the barn owl tends to restrict itself to small mammals and is therefore more vulnerable to the fluctuations of their prey species.

OWL CALLING

The call of the tawny owl is a familiar sound at night, and the two parts of the call are characterised in children's books as 'tu-whit tu-whoo'. It's not far off actually; the 'tu-whit' part of their call is made by both sexes, though more frequently by the female, but the tremulous hoot, the 'tu-whoo', is the male call. A resident pair will sometimes duet together, with the female squeezing in her contact call between the hooting of the male. There are a few ways to call owls, including replicating the territorial hoot using your cupped hands. It's important to pay close attention to the repetitive rhythm as well as the pitch of the call. In other words, copying the owls' pattern is key to attracting their attention. It begins with a drawn out 'hooo', followed by a short pause, then a softer 'hu' and a final phrase of 'huhuhuhooo', which has a strong vibrato quality.

Equipment required:
Owl whistle or recording of
owl calls (optional)
Torch
Sit mats (optional)
Ages: 6 and up
Number of participants:
2–30

It takes practise to convincingly reproduce an owl's call, but it's worth it. And even if there are no tawny owls around, it's a pretty neat trick to use as a gathering call for your family, friends or group.

The 'tu-whit' or 'ke-wick' call is not so easy. It requires a high falsetto voice and is a strain on the voice box, but it is possible to replicate the call exactly. I can do it, though it involves contorting my face into such a crazed expression that I tend to turn away from a group before sounding it, lest I frighten a small child.

A wooden owl whistle, often found in National Trust or zoo gift shops, is easy to use, and as long as you get the pattern and rhythm of the sound right, it is very effective. It can be operated using one hand, which is helpful if you need to carry equipment like a torch in your other hand.

Of course, if you are not device-averse, there are plenty of owl call recordings easily available to download onto a smartphone. Plugging a phone into a small speaker makes for a very accurate broadcast.

Now, I must tell you, the first time you try to call owls, you'll most likely fail. That's because, as with all good comedy, it's about getting the timing right. In other words, tawny owls are responsive only at certain times of the year; broadly speaking, spring, late autumn, and winter. Like most predators, owls are territorial and the males in particular need to advertise their presence. They do so intensely from March through to early May, depending on the region.

I like to make calling owls a perambulating activity – using my owl call when prompted by the owls themselves. When we hear a call, I stop the group and gather them close whilst I talk very quietly about the matter of owls whilst intermittently calling them in. Or, I ask the group to sit in a circle, which lends a sort of reverence to proceedings. A stand of mature deciduous trees is a likely place to encounter owls and provides good viewing potential.

The magic begins when there is a vocal response from a tawny owl (or more than one when its breeding season), and we can track its progress as it moves closer in to investigate the 'intruder' – me. Then we peer up through the branches where we will often see a flying silhouette, accompanied by a quavering 'on-the-wing' hoot. Thrilling enough. But the icing on the cake is to use a torch with a focused beam to illuminate the owl. Many will gasp at their first sight of these mysterious denizens of the night.

Should owls remain elusive, it's handy to have some props. I always carry a wing and a claw, or a skull that will stimulate interest. The wing is the perfect tactile illustration of how their soft, soft feathers help them fly so silently.

If you're not a nature educator, you probably don't carry wings and skulls in your pocket, but anyone can find an owl pellet to show. Owls excrete these pellets of indigestible residue two to twenty-four hours after eating. There's plenty about on the forest floor where owls are in residence, and because the pellets are not smelly or dirty, it always fascinates to break them apart to see the remnants of what they've been eating. It's usually possible, for example, to find a miniature jaw-bone, belonging to one of the small mammal prey items. It makes for a wonderful detective process to examine the jawbones to see the detail in the teeth of each species.

Notes

Please have consideration for owls during breeding time. Don't return to the same spot over and over to call owls, so that the same owls are not unduly disturbed. Also, use a torch beam that is not too fierce and, if you are successful and have a tawny owl in your sight lines, don't spend too long with them – one or two minutes is plenty of time for this experience.

About Bats

Old country names: shaky mouse, flying mouse, blind mouse,
bald mouse
Collective noun: colony

Bats can be found on every continent apart from Antarctica with about 1,400 different species of bat worldwide, making up roughly a fifth of all the species of mammals on Earth. The variations on bats as insectivores find them catching and eating fish in Asia and North America, eating fruit in the tropics and lapping up mammal blood in South America.

Despite the association of bats with all things dark and sinister, I find that people are delighted to see bats flitting about at dusk or dawn. There is something about this fascinating species that endears them to us, and local bat groups set up all over the country reflect this widespread interest and affinity.

These groups share a concern for the future of this amazing creature. Over the last one hundred years bat populations have fluctuated, threatened by habitat loss, declining numbers of roosting sites (such as old trees), disturbance from human development, intensified agriculture, timber treatment chemicals, predation by cats and more. All bat species are now protected by law, so it is an offence to disturb bats, or their roosts, which even if apparently abandoned may well be returned to. If you find an injured or orphaned bat, you are allowed to handle it for the purposes of rehabilitation, before contacting your local bat group, wildlife trust or the government's conservation organisation Natural England.

Nevertheless, bats are a common sight when we are out nightwalking or camping. Bats are active between April and October, and all our British species are nocturnal, echolocate and eat only insects. As diminutive predators, they have a high metabolic rate and so need to consume a lot of insects. Some species will eat between two and three thousand insects in a single summer night, almost equal to their bodyweight! They tend to favour visiting the same hunting grounds, so once you have identified where that is, you can expect to find your bats there, assuming the weather is conducive.

On windy, wet or cold nights there are fewer flying insects, so they don't feed, which is why they more than make up for it when conditions are favourable. And bats hibernate in winter, because there are few insects flying during those cold months.

Although traditionally a woodland dweller, bats can be found hunting in other types of areas. For example, the **noctule bat** hunts above the canopy, and the **Daubenton's bat** hunts over water. In fact, if you have access to a pond or lake, it can provide the most dramatic display of wild predator hunting action as the Daubenton's acrobats operate close to the surface where you will get a fantastic view. On a dark night, try viewing them using torches like follow-spots to track their dramatic flight path.

Here's some bat ecology to inform your bat presentations:

To dispel a popular myth, bats are not blind at all but can see at least as well as we do. But they couldn't hunt successfully in the dark if they relied on sight alone. Bats have therefore devised a solution whereby they send out sounds – a high-frequency echolocation system. They can capture information through the sound waves echoing back to them and so 'see' objects and hunt insects with deadly accuracy. Clever stuff!

Bats are nocturnal for a number of reasons, including avoiding predation and competition from birds who fly during the day. They can also overheat if they fly when the sun is strong.

Given the seasonal fluctuations in their food supply, it's not surprising that nature's genius has a design solution for reproduction to ensure the species is prolonged. Bats time their birthing of a single young to coincide with the availability of the food supply. In temperate zones, the female bat can store sperm in her body through hibernation, delaying fertilisation of an egg cell until the late winter/early spring. By May, when the pup is born, there's plenty to eat. The maternal bat will initially carry the infant whilst she feeds and as the young grow bat colonies will organise a 'creche' in the roosting site so that the parent bats can take it in turns to feed.

BAT AND MOTH

If ever there was a game that demonstrated learning whilst have fun, it would have to be Bat and Moth. Brought to us by that excellent practitioner of nature games, Joseph Cornell, this activity is a sure-fire way to galvanise a group's interest in these fascinating creatures. For maximum impact, draw out their curiosity first by playing Cornell's game of 'Noses' (see page 72).

For the safety of the players, choose a flat, even surface as the play area. Ask the group to gather in a circle and to stretch out their arms so that they can touch the fingers of those to either side. This provides enough of a 'hunting ground' without leaving gaps so wide that players might wander out of the circle.

Explain that in this game, one player is a 'bat' who tries to capture two 'moths' by echoloca-tion. Then ask if anyone can explain how echolocation works. When that has been made clear (either by a knowledgeable participant or by you), explain that this game mimics this natural process by using the human voices of the players for the same effect. (See About Bats on page 83 for an explanation of echolocation.)

> **Equipment required:**
> 3–4 blindfolds
> **Ages:** 8 and up
> **Number of participants:**
> 10–25

Ask for or select a volunteer to play the bat and two volunteers to be moths, and start with a little demonstration with those three players. Give clear instruction to play the game only at walking pace to reduce the risk of accidents. It's also a good idea to instruct the group to stretch their arms out to the side if any of the active players look like they might pass through the gap.

Rules

1. The bat is blindfolded and the moths are not. All three players must stay within the circle. The moths are trying to avoid detection. The bat is attempting to capture the moths.
2. Whenever the moths hear the bat shout 'bat!', they must respond immediately by shouting out 'moth!'.
3. The bat captures a moth by tagging that player – any contact will suffice.
4. When a moth is caught, the moth removes their blindfold and returns to the circle.
5. After the bat captures the second moth, another volunteer is chosen to be the bat and two more moth victims are also chosen.

As the game progresses, the learning about this complex mechanism of echolocation is embodied and embedded in an unforgettable way. It's hard not to enjoy the pantomime as the bat cavorts around, arms outstretched, trying to capture the prey – it's a comedy of errors for those watching the near-misses. As more players take part, an evolution of understanding unfolds as the demands of hunting by echolocation become more obvious.

Notes and Variants

A bat player may initially be unsuccessful, but be assured that bats soon learn that the more they use their voice, the more information they receive to help them locate their prey.

Choose carefully your first volunteers, particularly the bat, in order to have the game modelled well. Chaos can quickly descend if the first bat is intent on 'performing' to the crowd rather than trying to hunt effectively. If children are playing, it's best to choose an adult or an older/more sensible child as the first bat. Although this game does not preclude younger children, have your risk assessment antennae alert to the possible dangers of bumps and bruises that can ensue, especially from careless participants.

If you have a mature enough group, the capture of the moths can be when the bat holds onto the moths.

The game can be played with the moths blindfolded as well – it's a question of judgement in terms of the capacities of the players.

If the bat is an unsuccessful hunter, adjust the odds in the bat's favour by inviting everyone in the circle to take a step in, thereby making the hunting ground smaller and increasing the bat's chances.

BAT DETECTING

I can't think of a more exciting, sci-fi sounding bit of kit than a 'bat detector' and, believe me, the effect of producing one out of your nightwalk bag of props is dramatic. The best way to track the skies for bats out hunting at night is with a bat detector – see Bat Detectors in Chapter 2 for information on the various kinds of devices.

This is a jolly neat bit of kit that works by effectively lowering the sound frequencies that bats produce and amplifying them so that our human ears can hear them. Simply point the bat detector towards the bats. If you are dialled in to the range of frequencies emitted by the species you are looking for, you will be immediately rewarded with a responsive, percussive and mysterious sound coming from the little box in your hand. If it's too dark even to spot the bats' silhouettes, then simply scan around with the detector until it picks up their sound.

Equipment required:
Bat detector
Ages: 6 and up
Number of participants:
2–25

If you are a nature practitioner, it's wonderful to have more than one detector during a nightwalk so that they can be pointed in all directions to maximise the chance of success. The devices are so easy to operate even younger children can take a turn.

Notes

It seems that bats are unaffected by our human presence and so there is no danger of upsetting them. Indeed, a mass of body warmth can have the effect of attracting more insects, which means more prey for the bats.

It's best to avoid using a bat detector throughout hibernation season (November to April in the UK) because there is a risk of distracting them whilst they are trying to hunt during a time of diminished food supply. You won't see many bats during this season, but if you do, remember it's a lean time of year and if they are having to supplement their reserves to survive the winter, it's better to stay out of their way.

Of course it's possible to do a bit of bat detecting without investing in kit, you just need to be out in the twilight so that you can see them with the naked eye. Needless to say, you won't hear them but you can still observe them.

About Badgers

Old country names: brock, pate, grey, bawson
Collective noun: cete, clan

The badger is a loveable old rogue who has generally won the nation's affection, notwithstanding the antipathy of many farmers who feel threatened because badgers can be carriers of bovine tuberculosis that can also infect livestock. For the naturalist, however, to watch badgers being badgers is entrancing, not least because we are not often treated to their amusing antics.

The south west of Britain where I live is a particular stronghold for badgers, but they are generally widespread throughout the UK, though more rarely seen in Scotland and some parts of northern England.

Look for badger setts on south-facing, gentle slopes where there is some cover, for example in a wood, copse or hedgerow. Badgers typically prefer to excavate in sandy soils that are well drained and easy to dig.

Every badger clan has one main sett. These setts can become quite large over time: setts with a dozen to twenty or more entrances are common. Rabbits and foxes may take over disused setts. Look for the following signs of an active badger sett:

- Badger holes tend to be roughly south-facing, on an incline, and usually not too far from water.
  The entrance shape is about 20–30 cm (8–12 inches) wide and looks like a capital 'D'. Depending on the size of the clan, there may be just a few holes or there maybe more than a dozen. As a comparison, a fox digs a smaller, single hole unless it has occupied an old badger sett.
- Badgers sometimes leave a pile of old or fresh bedding material at the opening to the sett.
- Numerous shallow pits in the vicinity are a feeding sign, and indicate where badgers have been digging for earthworms, which are their main source of food.
- Badgers also dig shallow communal latrine pits a short distance from the sett. (Follow your nose to find these!)

- Claw marks can occasionally be found on nearby trees and fallen branches, or even rocks or fence posts.
- A good place to find/track them is where a badger trail crosses under a fence and leaves some traces of hair. Badger hair has black and white colouring as well as the 'square' feel when you roll it in your fingers and the crinkled appearance

Smell is the dominant sense for the badger, and it's an important social tool as well, to recognise the individuals from their own clan. There is a fierce rivalry between clan groups and so scent marking is employed to assuage any potential conflict. 'Musking' is a common practice, especially at mating times when dominant males will scent-mark sows. A subcaudal gland at the base of the tail produces a pale yellow fatty substance that is also used to mark trails in and around the sett.

You might be lucky enough to find a badger skull and there should be plenty about because their average life span is only three years (two thirds of badgers do not make it beyond their first year). You can distinguish it by noticing the hinge in the jaw. Chances are the lower jaw is still attached and this hinge helps to give the badger a powerful bite.

Badger claws are long, sharp and tough, and the animals are equipped with powerful shoulder muscles to dig deep into the earth. We may no longer feel the threat from fearsome predators in the British countryside, but a cornered or injured badger is armed with some lethal weapons and won't hesitate to use them if threatened, so beware!

There's plenty of old English folklore about badgers, including this sweet old rhyme from about two hundred years ago:

Should a badger cross the path
Which thou hast taken, then
Good luck is thine, so it be said
Beyond the luck of men.

But if it cross in front of thee,
Beyond where thou shalt tread,
And if by chance doth turn the mould,
Thou art numbered with the dead.

I would suggest, however, if a badger does 'cross in front of thee', then you are fortunate indeed and should be thrilled for the opportunity to observe one of our most unfamiliar, but favourite animals.

BADGER WATCHING

It may be that you bump into a badger as it bimbles about at night, but this would be a stroke of luck rather than something to rely on.

Equipment required:
Sit mats
Binoculars (optional)
Ages: 6 and up
Number of participants:
2–16

A 'bonus badger' has been a rare highlight on some of my solitary nightwalks, and even more so when I'm out with a group. Badgers can seem unfazed by humans, not noticing you if they haven't smelt you, intent on whatever potential food they are smelling. Once you draw close enough, they are suddenly alerted to your rather large and unexpected presence with pantomime surprise, rushing off into the dark.

After a quiet December when badgers are conserving fat supplies, they become more active during January as the breeding season approaches. February sees lots of activity as the males jostle for position, and the teenage boars are often expelled, leading to a sad flush of seasonal road deaths. Although mating can also be spread out throughout the year, birth is concentrated in February in order to take advantage of food availability. As with bats, this phenomenon of delayed implantation is an example of nature's intelligence and ability to adapt to its environment.

April is the magic month for watching badgers because it's when the cubs make their first appearance. The timing could not be better for nature lovers. As we sit outside in late April and early May hoping for a glimpse of young badgers, we are immersed in the vitality of a woodland in spring, drinking in the intoxicating bluebells, wood anemones and the first flush of fresh, tender green leaves. And what entertainment! The cubs are naïve, innocent, playful souls, and their behaviour is very affecting as they gambol about, falling off logs and play-fighting.

Watching badgers does require some fieldcraft skills, because they are a sensitive creature with a particularly keen sense of smell and good hearing. If you are organising a group badger-watch I recommend choosing a sett where there is a good viewing point for a group to gather comfortably and inconspicuously. For the best results, you might visit on successive days to bait the sett, being very careful not to leave your own scent trail too near the sett. For bait, use peanut butter, because peanut butter smeared on logs and stones lasts much longer than peanuts – it takes ages for the badger to lick it off! Make sure you get into position well before dusk and be prepared to wait. I would allow at least an hour and longer if you have the patience. If there is no sign, even well after dark, they have probably scented you. You will nevertheless have had an extraordinary experience of sitting quietly in the gathering dusk, and quite possibly you'll have perceived other natural phenomena such as bats or owls. Remember to leave as quietly as you can so as not to disturb.

Notes
Here are some other tips to bear in mind on a badger watch:

- Avoid brightly coloured clothing and 'noisy' waterproof clothing.
- Sit at least 10m away – the closer you are, the easier it is to be detected.
- Do not sit on the skyline where your outline would be conspicuous.
- Keep still to avoid making any noise.
- Sit in a place where you can feel the wind blowing from the sett towards you, i.e. downwind of the sett.
- Don't consume food or drink. The badgers will easily detect the unfamiliar smells and/or sounds of eating and drinking.
- Take binoculars to watch the badgers (they work well in the dark!) but so that you don't disturb them, be sure to remove the binoculars from their case before you arrive into your seat.
- Do not wear insect repellent because it will alert the badger to your presence. To avoid midges, cover all areas of exposed skin with hats/gloves/clothing.
- If there is no decent viewing platform near the sett, work out where the nearest water source is and position yourself to watch the badgers

make a beeline to quench their thirst. This is generally what they do first when they emerge from their sett.

About Moths

If butterflies are guilty of grabbing the limelight by day, then moths need a better PR agent to gain them more positive reviews. Let's start with the sheer numbers. There are 59 species of butterfly in Britain, which sounds a lot, but it pales into insignificance against the 2,500 species of moths that we enjoy on these enchanted islands.

Although there are plenty of nondescript 'little brown jobs', there is also a kaleidoscope of colour and character in the world of moths. As you will discover if you go out moth-trapping, the cast of characters in this nocturnal dumbshow can more than compete for colour and beauty with their diurnal cousins the butterflies. Moth colours represent the whole spectrum of the rainbow, and the creatures' appearance ranges from the cute to the bizarre.

Moths have been ascribed the most delicious names. Call them out loud and it has the feeling of some bardic poetic incantation:

Autumn green carpet, ruddy highflyer,
Canary-shouldered thorn,
Coxcomb prominent, dark dagger, dingy mocha,
Flounced chestnut, peach blossom,
Pale-brindled beauty, angle shades

There are excellent field guides to moths as well as smartphone apps for moth identification. To single out a few of our more charismatic species here, I will start with Britain's biggest, just because there is a tendency to veer towards extremes, and when things are generally small, size matters.

Clifden nonpareil. It has been bouncing back from UK extinction and can now be seen in southern England. Its impressive wingspan can reach 9.5cm (3.7 inches) and it bears a bright blue stripe across its black hind wings.

Hawk moths. These superbly patterned moths have muscular, heavy bodies. The elephant hawk-moth is lime green and sugar pink, and is so named because its caterpillar stage resembles an elephant's trunk.

Scarlet tiger moths. Some moths are also active during the daytime, and scarlet tigers are amongst that group. They draw attention by dramatically flashing their under wings as a warning to predators that they might not taste good. They also have caterpillars of distinction, being covered with protective, irritant hairs – the reason we call them 'woolly bears' and the reason the only birds to find them palatable are cuckoos.

Emperor moths. The distinctive set of four large eye-spots on the wings of emperor moths are not just eye-catching, but function to deter hungry birds. They also have impressive scent-catching equipment to detect the presence of females from 100 metres (328 feet) away. You can buy pheromone lures to attract this spectacular species.

Chinese character. This white moth qualifies for this selective list by having brown blotches, which helps it escape predation by impersonating a bird dropping.

Red sword-grass. With a head that looks like a shaven pencil, the red sword-grass moth could be confused with a broken-off birch twig.

There are also some species that evade capture by the voracious bats who zone in on moths using echolocation. Some tiger moths for example have evolved a sonar-blocking capacity to mask their whereabouts and to confuse the bats.

Overall, there is much to celebrate in shining a light on moths, with the only caveat to that being the general decline in numbers, of most concern being the alarming 40 per cent decrease in the south of the UK. It's an increasingly familiar story.

It's 'coming to light' that moths play a part in plant pollination. Recent investigation suggests they may play just as important a part in this crucial process as bees. Good news for moths, and all of us too, and it's bound to help them climb the priority species list for biodiversity issues.

MOTH TRAPPING

Moths are one of the more reliable species to encounter at night, and if you have the time and wherewithal, investing in a moth-trapping experience is a classic way to engender awe and wonder at what the natural world manifests at night.

There's something so intriguing about the appearance of what is normally hidden from view, and Britain's great diversity of moth species is one of our best-kept secrets.

High summer is the most productive time of the year for trapping moths. A simple construction of a container and a light to lure them is really all it takes. Set it up just before dusk and then the thrill of discovery follows – ideally the next morning. The moths are less active in the light of day and can be handled and observed more easily.

There are several types of commercially produced moth traps, as described in the Moth Traps section on page 39.

If you don't have a 'proper' moth trap, then improvise by stringing a rope or cord between two trees, hanging a white or light-coloured sheet over the line, and illuminating the sheet from behind with a lantern or torch. This creates a blank viewing canvas that will definitely attract moths.

At home you can even attract night-flying insects by leaving a light on in one room, the windows and curtains open to see what has come visiting. For closer observation you could carefully put one in a jam jar, which it won't mind for a short while. At least it's safe from bats in there.

And in case you were wondering, no one *really* knows why moths are so attracted by light. It's more presumed than proved that they use the moon's light to navigate and alternative theories abound but remain speculative. One I like is from a scientist called Philip S. Callahan who put forward his theory in the 1970s to explain why moths were lured into flames. The gist

Equipment required:
Moth trap or white/light-
    coloured sheet
Rope or cord
Torch
Ages: 8 and up
Number of participants:
2–25

of it was that the male moths were fooled by the light frequencies produced by candle flames, confusing them for the bioluminescent responses triggered by female moths' pheromones. In other words, this was an attempt to mate with the fire, a prospect that is always only going to end one way. It's no longer a theory to take too seriously, but don't you just love the mythotragic quality of this idea? Long live the mysteries of the night!

About Minibeasts

In the context of the wider natural balance, if ever there were unsung heroes, they are the minibeasts. These creatures are like the engine compartment of the natural world, and once you start removing components from what is driving the whole machine, then breakdown will surely follow. And talking of driving machines, you might recall if you are old enough the long car journeys made in the 60s and 70s that would always result in a great splattering of insects on the car windscreen and grill. How different it is today in Britain. I was reminded of how things 'should be' on a recent trip in Namibia when at the end of each day's drive the car would be comprehensively decorated. In a recent study in Germany by Caspar Hallmann it was found that the overall biomass of insects caught in 63 nature reserves fell by 75 per cent in the 27-year period from 1989 to 2014. Sobering stuff. If only they were cute and furry, we might give them a little more credit and a lot more wriggle room, so to speak.

One reason to learn about and seek out mini-critters is that they are always there. For three quarters of the year (outside of winter), they are reliable bit-part players in the whole nocturnal drama and can be depended upon to show up when other cast members fail to materialise. In other words, a minibeast safari will substantiate a nightwalk and yield instant mystery and surprise. When we operate our own 'follow-spot' (torch) to pick out what may be lurking beneath and outside our normal field of view, we find that intriguing things are going on, right under our noses. Narrative is an important part in this process; you have to be an 'invertebrate ambassador' and set the right tone, and tell the right stories. And boy, are there a lot of good stories to tell. I refer, of course, to the amazing life cycles that many insects have, and by plugging a few gaps in terms of their particular piece in the jigsaw of nature, it can lead to a whole lot more understanding and affinity.

Minibeast Diversity

The variety of minibeasts in Britain listed here is a glimpse into their incredible diversity, but this is by no means an exhaustive list of the little creatures that you might come across on a nocturnal safari. Take note, the numbers quoted here are also approximate, as definitive numbers are hard to establish due to factors including fluctuations and seasonal variations.

Ants: 36 species
Aphids and greenfly: 500 species
Beetles: 4,200 species
Centipedes: 41 species
Earthworms: 27 species
Earwigs: 4 species
False scorpions: 26 species
Harvestmen: 25 species
Land snails: 94 species
Millipedes: 53 species
Slugs: 29 species
Spiders: 647 species
Springtails: 300 species
Woodlice: 40 species

Some general jaw-dropping facts are always useful to have up your sleeve, and when it comes to insects there is no shortage.

- There are approximately 1.4 billion insects for every human alive.
- There are 51 native, terrestrial mammal species in the UK, but there are more than 4,000 species of beetle, approximately 9,000 species of wasps, and over 650 species of spiders.

- 75 per cent of crops in Europe require pollination by insects.

Some of the likely candidates to look for on a nightwalk are harvestmen, woodlice, beetles, spiders, centipedes, millipedes, slugs and land snails. With the exception of the rarer glow-worms, most will be found all over the British countryside, lurking in the undergrowth.

Glow-worms

Collective noun: glimmer (an interesting exception here: the prescription of a rare collective noun for insects)

Top of the bill in this diminutive cast of characters, if you can find them, must be the remarkable glow-worm, which, it turns out, is not a worm at all but a beetle. Glow-worms are the celebrities of the invertebrate world, and a sheer delight to discover on the trail. The female of the species does not fly and uses complex compounds and chemical reactions to produce light energy from a light organ at the base of her abdomen, which is emitted to attract mates who are equipped with wings to fly about in the dark looking for this mini landing strip. These tiny greenish lights low to the ground are what to look out for in summertime, and there can be dozens of them clustered together. Because this mating ritual is only about 2 per cent of the female's life-cycle, you can understand why it's such a marvel to stumble across it.

Glow-worm larvae can travel along the ground at about 5 metres per hour, fast enough to hunt down slugs and snails, which they will attack despite being a fraction of their size. The glow-worm larva is equipped with a poison that it endeavours to inject into the 'foot' of the slug or snail. It's a precision task, but if successful the larva will follow, sometimes riding the shell of a snail, until the toxin begins to digest the innards of the prey, which can then be lapped up by the larva. Such a huge meal necessitates the larva to undergo several moultings in a 15-month period until it's ready to pupate.

Light pollution in its many forms now confuses the mating operation, making it much harder for the females to locate their potential mates. Likewise, the decline of meadows and grasslands has also impacted populations. So you are fortunate indeed these days to have glow-worms in your area. But if you do, they add some X factor to the night's enchantment.

Harvestmen

Appearances can be deceptive, I don't know how many times I've said this to nightwalk participants, who make fair assumptions about these compelling creatures, but for the record, they aren't spiders!

Spiders have two body parts whereas harvestmen appear to have only one due to its two body segments being largely fused together. The scientific name for harvestmen, which are also sometimes called 'daddy longlegs,' is Opiliones and, unlike spiders, they don't have a venomous bite and they don't spin webs.

But they are compelling, moving about at night in their strange suspension (their bodies 'suspend' in the air), like something out of a Tim Burton movie. Their legs have seven segments, with the front pair being more for sensory exploration than locomotion. Don't be fooled by their fairy-like appearance, for they are predators as well as scavengers, often attacking larger insects that are ill or damaged – they will even feed on the dead (insects, that is…)!

Woodlice

Old country names: armadillo bugs, cheese logs, pill bugs

Reliably found in the dark and damp recesses under rotting logs and loose tree bark, these fourteen-legged little charmers are in fact a land crustacean rather than an insect. But their strangeness doesn't stop there. In fact, they are little trundle bundles of particular peculiarity. For example, their breathing is done through gills and requires a moist environment to function whilst they go about their business composting dead plant material and fungal growths. Another endearing fact (not!) is that they eat their own faeces, but don't actually urinate. Instead, they produce then expel ammonia through their shells. And just as you are pausing for breath, it gets even weirder: they have blue blood and they drink through their bums! They are also rather marsupial in possessing a brood pouch in which to carry their fertilised eggs. One last bizarre feature to cap it all, is that if the males become infected with a particular type of bacteria, they change into females.

Beetles

Good gracious! How many? Pity the entomologist whose task may be to catalogue and remember their names. So many of our insects don't have common names, but those that do tend to be, well, more common. Many beetles will be revealed under stones and rotten bark, which should always be carefully replaced, but under the torch spotlight all sorts of beetle activity can be seen down on the ground and on the trees. So many beetle narratives to spin on a nightwalk whenever you come across them. For example, **blister beetles** secrete cantharidin, something that can be poisonous to humans. Males give cantharidin to the to females during mating, who use it to cover their eggs as a defence against predators. We use it in diluted form to treat warts and remove tattoos.

There are five species of **oil beetle** in the UK and they share the characteristic of secreting oil when alarmed. Even though they aren't strictly nocturnal, if there's one story you've got to tell about invertebrates, it's this one, as it's so extraordinary:

Many thousands of larvae hatch from the eggs of a female oil beetle, who lay them in the earth of their burrows. The larvae are programmed to find and ascend the closest stalks, where they wait in the flowers to catch a ride to their next destination from a solitary bee. They have specially adapted claws to hitch themselves on and, when they arrive at the bee's nest or burrow, they help themselves to its eggs and pollen. After pupation, they emerge in beetle form the next spring.

Now, after a story like that, I find myself wondering how on earth did that all begin...?

Spiders

If you suffer from arachnophobia, you may not be happy to learn that there are so many species of spider in Britain, and that you may find them almost everywhere at night. But most are tiny and although all are poisonous to their prey, they don't harm us. An exception to this is the bite of the **noble false widow spider**, which has caused some severe and painful reactions, but such stories are overblown by the media as this is very rare. The bacteria on the spider's palps (extra-tactile appendages between the legs and the mouthparts) will cause an allergic reaction accompanied by a stinging sensation. This non-native spider has colonised the south coast, and I've been bitten by it myself. I didn't notice the bite at first, but then my foot swelled up like a proverbial balloon (it was successfully treated with antibiotics).

Apart from the noble false widow, our spiders present a fascinating diversity of beings, from the rare but alarmingly chunky **fen raft spider**, which spans a human palm, to the water spider – the only spider in the world to live almost exclusively underwater courtesy of air bubbles it collects on the hairs on its legs.

Centipedes

As the old joke goes, what goes 99-clunk, 99-clunk? Answer: a centipede with a wooden leg. Despite that punchline, our UK species can have as many as 202 or as few as 30 legs. These busy, energetic predators are similar to but entirely separate from millipedes. A centipede will hunt down anything that it can overcome. This voracious hunter is also equipped with 'leg claws' at the front, which are what deliver the strong poison. Perhaps their most curious attribute, though rare to find, is the capacity of at least three species of centipede to emit bioluminescence. Curious because centipedes are effectively blind and it's not known for sure why this curious phenomenon exists. The most plausible explanation is that the light, which is usually produced after a centipede is stimulated with touch, must be part of its defensive armoury.

Like most ground-dwelling nocturnal invertebrates, they will be found skulking about in amongst the leaf litter, and in and around decaying wood.

Millipedes

Two pairs of legs attached to each body segment is one of the ways to identify a millipede, but in general they have shorter legs than centipedes. They also move at a much more relaxed pace, lifting each pair of legs with a graceful 'wave' motion.

This class of arthropods is thought to be amongst the first animals to have colonised land 443 million years ago.

They are detritivores – animals that feed on decomposing organic material, including faeces – and so are another helpful piece in the composting matrix. They are preyed upon by all sorts of insectivores but many have a defence strategy that includes rolling up into a ball and/or secreting a caustic liquid that can have a corrosive effect on their insect predators.

In their bizarre reproductive process, **bristly millipede** males spin a web on which they deposit their sperm. The female then approaches the web and puts the sperm into her own reproductive organs. But in other pill millipede species, a male attracts a female to mate with squeaking noises made by rubbing the bases of his legs against his body. He then grasps the female's body with his legs, releases a sperm packet behind his head and uses its legs to pass the packet back from one pair of legs to the next, until it reaches the reproductive organs of the female. Another pill millipede species gets properly dirty, as this same process can't take place until the male has covered his packet with soil before delivering it to his sweetheart. Whatever turns you on I suppose…

Earwigs

The charmingly named earwig is another nocturnal scavenger that retreats to rest in rotten logs or under stones by day, and can be found anywhere and everywhere at night.

Unusually for insects, the female of the **common earwig** is an excellent mother. After laying her eggs in damp nooks and crannies, she guards the nest and gently cleans the eggs until the young hatch. She then keeps guard until the babies – called nymphs – are ready to fend for themselves.

The fearsome-looking pincers at the rear end of the common earwig can deliver a nip to humans, but they are generally used to scare off predators, a case of their bark being worse than their bite.

It is said that the name earwig comes from the (false) claim that they climb into people's ears at night, but in fact the name arises from the shape of their hind wings that were once called 'ear wings'.

Earthworms

Just because these are out of sight, they should not be out of mind. These subterranean, dark-loving creatures are bound to be unearthed in your general ground-rummaging in the leaf litter.

Earthworms are detritivores like earwigs and digest dead organic material, breaking it down so that bacteria and fungi can feed on it. These decomposers then convert this matter into the nutrients that plants need to grow. Thus, it's not surprising earthworms have been referred to as the 'ecosystem engineers'. Indeed, it was Darwin's enthusiastic view that their effect on soil structure made them 'nature's ploughs', and so let's hear it for another of our unsung heroes. Many parents will tell you about their toddler's natural affinity with worms, and most will find there is something endearing about these wriggling, writhing, wee beasties.

And as if that wasn't enough to justify their crucial place in the great ecological scheme of things, then let's not forget how many species depend upon the humble earthworm as a food source – badgers, foxes, moles, hedgehogs, shrews and many birds to name but a few.

Slugs

Even though they don't sting us, bite us or suck our blood, slugs may never win a minibeast popularity contest, but that does not make them any less fascinating. On a nightwalk, slime trails glinting in the moonlight are a giveaway sign of slugs. Because of this mucousy excretion, slugs lose water rapidly and that's why they are active in the cool, moist conditions of night. Their slime reduces friction, 'greasing' the way to make them more efficient travellers, as well as being a deterrent to predators. There's no doubt that when you handle slugs the slime is unpleasant and hard to remove from your hands afterward. Scientists are still trying to figure out how slug slime, which is only mildly sticky at first, changes to become like a quick-drying cement when it's left on the trail. There may be some useful applications for humans if we can replicate a slug's slime formula.

Slugs have a voracious appetite for plants and they are an important part of the great decomposition story, but did you know that slugs have as many as one hundred thousand teeth on its tongue-like radula? Or, that a few species are covered in prickles, like the **hedgehog slug**? Or, that the largest slug in the world is resident in the UK and can reach an impressive 25cm (10 inches) long?

The sex lives of slugs are somewhat astonishing. In many slug species, the penis is about half the size of its body, an impressive fact to share on a nightwalk with a group of teens or adults. When slugs are on heat, they secrete a chemical in their trail of slime, which helps them find each other. Seductive foreplay then takes place where each explores and samples the chemical secretions on the surface of the other. Most slugs possess both male and female sex organs, and the eventual insemination is reciprocal. Occasionally, their slime is a little too adhesive and when the pair's organs become stuck together, one will gnaw off the other's penis in a process called apophallation. The one that is dispossessed continues on their way to live life as a female.

The onslaught of slugs in the garden testifies to flourishing populations and to maintain these levels slugs can also self-fertilise if mates are in short supply.

Best learn to love 'em, cos you ain't gonna stop 'em!

Land Snails

Similar in many ways to their slug cousins, but with much better PR; snails do the same sort of damage to plants, but at least offer themselves to be more appetising in exchange. In fact in some parts of the world, people also eat snail eggs, calling it 'white caviar'. Other 'benefits' from snails are more medicinal, with the mucus of the garden snail used to treat wrinkles, spots and scars on the skin.

Using an average, snails can move along at an electrifying 15mm per second, which means that if they moved without stopping it would take more than a week to complete one kilometre.

MINIBEAST SAFARI

Minibeasts do not generally sell themselves well, and in my experience, putting in a bit of extra effort to engage a group's interest and curiosity in this activity is well worthwhile. Below is an example of how I might lead a minibeast safari, but feel free to dream up your own angle for encouraging your group to get down in the dirt to find some beasts.

'Hey, you lot! Check this out!' I back up this invitation by holding up something in my cupped hands – something that cannot immediately be seen. As a few people start to crowd around me, others inevitably become curious.

When all are gathered, I open my hands slowly, revealing the small box or bag. As everyone watches and wonders what is inside, I open the box and reveal a mysterious green light. It's unexpected and intriguing, and so the question immediately follows… 'What is that?'

This is a grand way to introduce one of the night-time's most beguiling creatures, the glow-worm. It's an easy sell because this radiant being is a card-carrying member of nocturnal nature's celebrity club. Although they have become a rare find, they are one of the most reliable invertebrates to capture a group's appreciation and attention. After a bit of narrative storytelling (see Glow-worms on page 97) to heighten the group's interest, introduce the idea of the night-time being a safe haven for insects. It's the perfect opportunity to go on a nocturnal safari to make some discoveries!

Equipment required:
Cloth bag (not plastic, please!)
Mini torches (ideally with coloured filters over the lens)
1 tiny glow stick or 'fisherman's light' placed inside a small box or bag
Ages: 6 and up
Number of participants: 4–25

When the storytelling is complete, ask the group if they would like to form a hunting party and to divide into pairs. Now offer a very special invitation: to go and search for creatures they have never seen before. They can be found in all sorts of out-of-the-way places like in rotten wood, under rocks, on tree trunks, the underside of leaves or in the shallows of stream beds.

Out of the cloth bag comes a heap of little torches that have been adapted with a coloured filter adhered to the glass, to produce a coloured beam of light with which to hunt minibeasts. How kids love props! This is all it takes to get them excitedly on the trail, tempted with the further thrilling prospect of making a brand new discovery of some hitherto undiscovered insect. Everyone likes to leave their mark in the world and I playfully suggest they could make conservation history and lend their name to a creature that is new to science.

As I hand out torches, I say something like, 'We are merely visitors to this other world and we must move quietly if we are to be successful in the hunt. But if you see something interesting out there you want to share, rather than disturbing the peace by calling out, flash your torch on and off instead to invite other hunters to take a look at your discovery.' Be sure to give instructions regarding taking care of the habitats and creatures encountered – don't peel off rotten bark to see what's underneath and be sure to replace any stones that have been lifted up.

Whilst the group are hunting, it's important to go on your own safari too – not just to model with your own curiosity, but also to increase the yield of discoveries. A short 15 minutes on this trail can be very fruitful, particularly in the abundance of late spring and summer. Even autumn continues the rich harvest. This is how invertebrates triumph over other creatures, in their sheer volume and diversity. There's always a surprise to find, and the finale of the activity is to call everyone in and find out what was discovered – usually a long list of species, many of which have to be described because the names are unknown (so be sure you study up a bit in advance, too).

To finish up, gather in the torches, and underline the wonder and mystery of nocturnal nature with some final dramatic statements. You might reveal the staggering number and diversity of invertebrates, for example, and describe how pivotal they are in the ecosystem.

About Foxes

Old country names: Tod, Reynard
Collective noun: skulk or leash

Br'er Fox turns up reliably any time of the year, by day as well as during their more active time through the night. Not so easy to find them in the countryside though, where they are much more circumspect than urban foxes, which some people report are 'ten a penny' if you are in the habit of walking or driving through big cities at night. Fox populations have been difficult to quantify and there is no definitive census figures, but it's thought to have declined in rural Britain, but increased significantly in cities, where they were first reported in the 1930s.

Wintertime can be fruitful for finding foxes. Just as many turn their attention towards the visit of Santa, this other red-coated visitor shows up in the dark, sometimes with a strange blood-curdling scream. This is the vixen, advertising her presence to any potential dog fox in the vicinity, who gives a 'bow-wow-wow' bark in response. The window for mating is brief, as the vixen will be receptive for only two to three days. Make a note in your diary that seven to eight weeks after this, the cubs will be born.

Although the fox is the most widespread member of the *Canidae* family (which also includes dogs and wolves) ranging from the arctic to the desert, its most unusual characteristic is its ability to retract its claws, like a cat. Foxes share another attribute with their feline cousins: their eyes have that same vertical pupil, enabling them to adapt to both light and dark conditions.

Unlike cats, foxes have a wide range of vocalisations – at least twenty different call types have been recorded. The most notorious of these is the vixen advertising her presence to a mate, which in *The Wood in Winter* nature writer John Lewis-Stempel poetically described as 'The wail of all the bereaved.'

A fox's diet will stretch to include berries, worms, spiders, beetles, and small animals such as mice and birds, and they hunt predominantly by sound. Research also suggests they have an orientation to the Earth's magnetic field, which, in combination with their hearing, enables them to pounce on and capture small mammals they cannot see.

One of the tell-tale signs that foxes are in the vicinity is a distinctive acrid smell that hangs in the air which comes from their habit of marking the borders of their territory with urine.

Other evidence left behind are their droppings, often strategically placed around territory boundaries, on raised ground and with the characteristic twisted, tapered end, full of fur, bone fragments and fruit pips, depending on the bounty of the season. You might also find their den (also called an earth) if you are roaming off the beaten track. Foxes also commonly occupy abandoned badger holes or enlarge a rabbit's burrow. The vixen will sometimes move her cubs if she feels threatened, so be very respectful in early spring in case you disturb a fox family. And just so you are aware, they are not legally protected, but it is against the law in England and Wales to hunt them with dogs, since the Hunting Act was passed in 2004.

Foxes as wily tricksters have figured prominently in a wide variety of literary sources from the Ancient Greeks to Aesop's fables, and more generally in films, songs and dances. There are at least 315 pubs bearing 'fox' in their name within the UK, and so next time you're in one of them, raise a glass to this fine old friend of ours.

NOCTURNAL SOUNDSCAPE

Even a simple guessing game can offer intrigue when the clues include some of the more unnerving sounds of nocturnal creatures. The sounds of fallow or red deer rutting, for example, are definitely unsettling to those who aren't familiar with them. The scream of a fox in its midwinter breeding season can sound like some awful murderous act, and the hoarse screeching call of the barn owl is ghostly and haunting.

That's the basic premise of this game. Get outdoors in the dark, play a recording of an animal or bird call, and ask the group to guess what creature it is they're hearing. This heightens curiosity, presents an opportunity for some information and questions, and adds a dimension of naturalist science to a nightwalk.

> **Equipment required:**
> Smartphone or digital
>   recording device
> Mini speakers (optional)
> **Ages:** 6 and up
> **Number of participants:**
> Any

It's now very easy to equip yourself with the recordings of nocturnal nature to play out loud using a smartphone or digital recorder and, if you wish, a small speaker. You can find these sounds on various phone apps, or take some nightwalks in advance so you can record animal and bird calls yourself using a digital recorder or the voice recorder on your smartphone. You can even stream recordings of sounds direct from the internet, assuming you have connection. (Note: this is always a bit risky outdoors.)

In terms of our cast of characters for this 'radio play', the list is long. It's a good idea to make your selection in advance so that this game doesn't become too drawn out. I suggest you capture the communication calls and cries of the following nocturnal species so that you have them downloaded onto your device ready to go.

Mammals: fox, badger, red deer, fallow deer, roe deer, wild boar, hedgehog, bats (including the horseshoe species) and otter.

Birds: tawny owl, barn owl, long-eared and short-eared owls, nightjar, corncrake, curlew and nightingale.

And, just for fun, and to play a bit more on our collective fear of the dark, how about the howl of the wolf or the growl of a big cat!

More Creature Facts and Lore

In many ways, Britain is impoverished when it comes to mammals, with only 51 species of terrestrial, native residents, living in a denuded landscape. But if we widen our scope and look for all the other nocturnal animals we have, we can feel enriched by a wonderful menagerie of creatures that may be encountered.

Hedgehogs

Old country names: hotchi-witchi (old Roma nickname)
Collective noun: prickle, snuffle, array

The hedgehog wins hands down in the Britain's Got Wild Talent favourite animal stakes. It's not common to stumble across them on your night perambulations, but if you do, the cute-ometer is high, and it's a delight to meet this living breathing cartoon character snuffling about in the dark.

Its habit of showing up in our gardens probably helps its cause in endearing itself to the British nation, and a BBC *Wildlife* magazine poll in 2016 for Britain's favourite wild animal revealed that it won with 42 per cent of the votes! That's a landslide majority in political terms, and credit is surely due to the PR department of the *Saving Britain's Hedgehogs* TV series.

Hedgehogs are insectivores and eat a variety of grubs and beetles, but will also take carrion given the chance. They also exhibit some bizarre behaviour. Before you cry 'fake news' at these revelations, please understand that these are confirmed reports that you can confirm yourself on YouTube if you don't believe me.

Self-anointing involves the hedgehog covering its spines with a frothy saliva-stimulant mixture, a behaviour that can last a few minutes or a few hours. What is interesting is that nobody really knows what it's all about. There are a number of theories that include grooming, scent marking or predator evasion, but none are conclusively established. Yet another wildlife mystery prevails.

Hedgehogs also engage in the even more confounding practice of walking or running in circles. I mean, they have been observed for hours, not minutes! Whilst it's easy to jump to the conclusion that something must be 'wrong' with the creature, it seems to happen with apparently healthy animals.

As far as I know, no hedgehog has ever been observed displaying both these strange behaviours at the same time.

There is more solid natural history to fall back on and here are a few choice titbits from the life and times of our most beloved, but sadly declining, hedgehog.

- Hedgehogs will hibernate in colder weather, but in parts of Europe with a warmer climate they tend not to.
- They make summer nests of lighter construction and warmer ones for winter. They have little nest fidelity, however.
- The annual hedgehog rut takes place over the summer, which means hoglets can be born as late as the autumn in a second litter for the sow, but peak time for births is June/July.
- Seven thousand renewable spines will deter most predators, though badgers have found a way to open this prickly puzzle.
- Despite it not being a social animal, the hedgehog produces a wide vocabulary of sound, including rather unnerving screams when being attacked. Also, expect whistles, clucks, snorts, huffs and the 'twitter' of the hoglets.
- UK data proposes they live only five to six years on average in the wild, though more recent data from Denmark found one individual to be sixteen years old.

Deer

Collective noun: herd

Depending how far back in time you look, there is credence given to either two or three native species of deer. The **fallow deer** were certainly reintroduced by the Normans, though evidence points to a more ancient heritage. The **roe** and the **red deer** have been here continuously, and the latter is now

Britain's largest terrestrial mammal. There's something about deer that captures our hearts, whether it be their sailing-boat grace and gentleness of the females, or the full-blooded va-va-voom of the stags during the rut. When going to look for deer, something primordial is galvanised within me, as if some ancestral hunter's blood is stirred, even though I'm only going for some quiet observation. It's not simply that bigger is better, but there is a great satisfaction in observing the larger terrestrial animals at close quarters.

Though not strictly nocturnal, deer are abroad at night, but especially at dusk and dawn. However, you'll need your wits about you to spend any quality time with them as they are well equipped to outwit and outpace your efforts to observe them. They see well, they have an excellent sense of hearing and they can smell your approach well before you arrive.

Getting to know the regular haunts and rhythms of the deer in your area is much to your advantage before taking a group for a deer observation experience. It's not necessary to become some sort of ninja stalker for success. Wearing the right clothing, paying attention to wind direction, and employing stealth and patience will reap rewards. Look first for signs of feeding or resting. In the woods, watch for lightly flattened areas or shallow depressions, called lie-ups, where they will spend time on the ground chewing the cud; also look for trees with bark stripped off. It's easy to find well used deer trails, and the presence of plenty of droppings indicates a good area to sit nearby and wait.

During the autumn rut, deer are much easier to find, especially in open country like the moorlands. You'll hear them more often than you see them and the two largest UK species, red deer and fallow deer, offer a testosterone-fuelled soundtrack to the season, with guttural groans and bellows reverberating throughout the night, bringing those stories of the 'beast' on the moors to mind. The male roe deer, however, has a very different vocalisation. Many a time I've been jolted awake in my hammock at night by its startling dog-like bark close by, often followed by the percussion of departing hoof beats.

Easier views are afforded of red deer as they emerge from the coombes and valleys and onto the moors to broadcast their virtues and fight with other males. It's a thrilling event in the wildlife calendar, especially with the stunning backdrop of Exmoor and the Highlands in their autumn palette of colour.

More widespread throughout Britain, and dwelling in the residues of our woods and copses, roe deer have been a consistent presence for a long time, and although they had been hunted to near extinction they are currently undergoing a revival, with flourishing populations. These are smaller deer that you tend to see in ones and twos, whereas fallow you will see in small herds in the wild or in larger herds in parks and estates. Roe deer have short antlers and a brown to red coat, turning greyer in winter, while fallow deer have larger flat (palmate) antlers and can range in colour from dark brown to beige with the classic dappled spots on their backs.

Three other deer species have been introduced and now live feral in parts of Britain: the sika deer, Chinese water deer and the diminutive **muntjac** deer.

Otters

Old country names: tarka, water snake, water dog, dratsie (Scottish)
Collective noun: romp

It's highly unlikely you'll see an otter on a nightwalk, but they are nevertheless on the guest list of our soiree with Britain's nocturnal wildlife, and what a thrill should you be lucky enough to see one.

Otters operate like ghost assassins of the night, easily evading our attentions as they busy themselves around the rivers and wetlands. On quieter nights, you might hear some otter vocalisations expressed in whistles and squeaks, growls, grunts and chirps.

I see the non-endemic mink more regularly on the riverbank, and these well-adapted cousins are often confused for otters. One most obvious difference is the larger size and musculature of the otter, with its chunky tail, used as both a swimming aid as well as a defensive weapon.

The otter hunts of old persecuted the poor miscreant and this together with habitat destruction and the indiscriminate use of harmful pesticides drove otter populations close to extinction in England. Thankfully, otters are now protected and thriving again after the banning of certain pesticides.

Strictly speaking, otters are not nocturnal, but have a preference for the peace and quiet of the river at night. In England particularly, where most of the persecution took place, they are more sensitive to disturbance. I count myself lucky to have had a number of sightings on the rivers of England

and more reliably in Scotland, where they have adapted to the coastline very successfully.

The otter is not confined to rivers, foraging far and wide in field, marsh and wetland to satisfy what is a voracious appetite for eels, frogs, birds, insects, molluscs and crustaceans.

Otters are members of the *Mustelidae* family, along with badgers, weasels and stoats. They are a particularly sleek bit of design by Mother Nature. Not only can they swim like a fish (well, better actually, because if they didn't, they couldn't catch them!), they can hold their breath for up to eight minutes underwater.

The quality of their fur is also legendary for its unique thickness and warmth. Underneath an otter's fur there is an additional layer of very thin hairs that can trap air. It's this bit of design genius that enables otters to maintain their body temperature in harsh conditions.

The pups whilst very young have particularly dense fur that will keep them afloat in the water, but which does not allow them to swim underwater. Within ten weeks they are adept at swimming but stay connected to the family group to be mentored in hunting until they are fully weaned and separate at six months.

Like with most wildlife, and especially the elusive kind, the best way to evidence their presence in a river system is go looking for signs. This mostly means their distinctive droppings left in quite conspicuous places. Look for the 'smudge-style' spraint (droppings) on rocks or fallen trees, or anywhere exposed on the river. To verify your suspicions, make sure you smell it. If it's from an otter, it will smell fishy, and even kind of sweet. It has been compared to jasmine tea, though I think that's stretching it. You should also see residual fish bones in the spraint because this makes up around three quarters of their diet.

Nightjars

Old country names: scissors grinder, goatsucker, dorr-hawk, wheel bird, churn owl, fern owl, flying toad

One of the weirdest nature experiences available derives from this strange but alluring bird. A brief visitor for breeding from the African continent, it makes its dramatic entrance onto our wildlife stage in May, announcing itself with its distinctive and distinctly odd churring call between dusk and dawn. Suddenly vanishing in August, it must have puzzled many in the past and present times. In olden times in the Westcountry and Europe, such was the mystery and intrigue around its sudden appearance and disappearance, they attributed the blame to the nightjar for stealing the milk from the udders of the goats. And because it was the villain of the piece, it was charmingly known as the 'goatsucker', preserved in its Latin name '*caprimulgus europaeus*'.

You'll find the nightjar on heathlands, moorlands and in areas of clear fell where it looks for cover from heather or bracken for nesting sites. It begins its monotonous territorial call after sunset, but you'd be hard-pressed to locate the perched bird from sound alone as it's like an act of ventriloquism and, combined with its mottled, tawny plumage, will confound getting a visual on it. Best look for the birds in flight. Its scissor-like wings and bat-like flight makes it easy to spot at dusk, the flight often accompanied by a sudden 'gwick' sound as they wheel about the darkening skies hurtling after moths, their mouths agape.

Naturalist author and presenter Nick Baker showed me a clever nightjar hunting trick on Trendlebere Down on Dartmoor one sultry May evening, to the astonishment of our accompanying group. To mimic the display flight of the male nightjar, which ends with a few audible wing-flaps, you stand in a conspicuous place out in the open, and with two white tissues/handkerchiefs, one in each hand, you raise your arms up and down, and then clap your hands. This is also then a visual prompt and replicates the white glimpses of the nightjar's under wings. It sounds rather far-fetched but it does have the desired effect of attracting the birds at the height of their breeding season. Magical birds require magical practices!

Other 'Nocturnal' Birds

There are many species of birds that, whilst not strictly nocturnal, are either crepuscular (active at twilight), or can be activated into nocturnal feeding by the light of a good moon or by sheer necessity. These include wildfowl like **ducks** and **geese**, and wading birds. Warblers like the **reed** and **sedge warblers** can be heard singing lustily late into the evening.

Many nights camped out on the riverbank and estuary I have enjoyed a concert of bird voices especially **shelducks**, **oystercatchers** and the **curlew**, whose haunting and beautiful call is the abiding soundtrack of wonderful canoe adventures on the river Dart.

The other obvious character amongst nocturnal birds is the **nightingale**. However, contrary to widespread assumptions, it is not strictly nocturnal, but the territorial male is sometimes heard singing in the night – though his song is often confused with that of a robin, who competes very well as a fellow songster. Given the widespread decline of the former, the chances are that when you think you are being treated to arias from a nightingale, it is probably a robin's serenade you are enjoying.

One bird who can't be confused with any other is the **corncrake**. Another species that has suffered a serious decline due to modern agricultural practice, the corncrake is clinging on in the north of Scotland. Its distinctive and repetitive 'crake-crake' call from dusk till dawn gives the bird its name. Despite its moniker, it is not confined to cornfields, preferring shorter crops it can see over.

I also like to include nocturnal migrants in a list of birds to look and listen for. Many of these travel by night, navigating by the stars, and their contact calls can often be heard way up above. During the autumn for example, listen for the 'seep-seep' calls of **redwings** and **fieldfares** coming in from Scandinavia for our milder winter, as do many geese heading South to our estuaries, lakes and fens from the Arctic.

Newts, Frogs and Toads

All our newts, frogs and toads are by and large nocturnal, on account of the need to avoid the desiccating effect of daylight.

Despite their strong association with and dependence on water, these creatures aren't always found in or around pools and ponds, preferring the sanctuary of damp, shady places offered by holes, logs and rocks. Breeding takes place in water but generally they live on land. They feed on slugs, snails, spiders and worms, all foods more reliably found at night.

Amongst the first events to herald the dawning of a new wildlife year is easily discovered by heading out at night with a torch to find one of nature's 'men's groups' gathering together for some purring and posturing before the arrival of the females. No, it's not a Friday night in a market town pub, but a scene from your local pond. Male frogs congregate as early as January in the south of England, and a mass of frogspawn is soon to be seen in ponds and ditches and even puddles. Toad spawn follows later, and is easily distinguished from frogspawn by their string-like shapes. The phenomenon of writhing masses of frogs and toads returning to the ponds of their birth is one of the early natural spectacles in the calendar year. When the females do arrive the desperate males compete for the privilege of mating, croaking for their attention and hoping they have the necessary X factor to attract a female. The process that follows is called amplexus.

The male leaps onto the back of the female and hang on for dear life, often for up to twenty-four hours, thereby positioning themselves to externally fertilise the eggs as soon as they are dispatched by the female. This level of wild enthusiasm is rather inelegantly expressed as more than one male will fight for the dominant position. Males will mate with different females on successive nights, and as soon as the breeding has finished, usually by early May, they will leave the ponds, and the eggs, to their own fate.

Nature's law of plenty applies to the sheer volume of frog and toad spawn, and up to two thousand eggs in a raft of spawn can be seen en masse – and it is eagerly consumed by fish and birds that haunt the same habitats. Note that you should not move frogs or frog spawn from one pond to another to avoid spreading a virus known as red-leg (due to its symptoms) that has hit them.

Our **common frog** is our main native species, but recently the **pool frog** has re-established itself in East Anglia. There are also some exotic species that have settled in some isolated regions of the UK. These are the **edible frog** and **marsh frog**.

If you are unsure how to distinguish frog from toad, give it a gentle nudge. Although both species can move in both ways, frogs tend to hop and toads generally prefer to walk or crawl, on shorter legs. Toads have a noticeably drier, warty skin compared to the sleek and shiny complexion of frogs, which can also lighten or darken to blend in with their environment.

Unlike a lot of amphibian species, **common toads** are quite happy in ponds that have fish; unlike frog tadpoles, toad tadpoles are toxic to fish. They continue to be able to secrete toxins as adult toads and therefore have fewer predators, though they will still be eaten by herons, crows and grass snakes.

All amphibians do a version of hibernation between October and March, though some scientists will use the term 'brumation' to describe the period that is not necessarily without some activity. Toads and frogs will bury themselves wherever the temperature is stable and there is some moisture content, for example a compost heap, though frogs will sometimes choose the rather risky location buried in the mud under the water of ponds, which of course is precarious due to the potential of a winter freeze.

Because toads breed just a little later than frogs, from March onwards, the toadlets usually emerge from ponds a little later too, during the month of August.

Although the common toad is widespread in Britain, its population is currently in decline. The **natterjack toad** is much rarer, confined to coastal sand dune systems, coastal grazing marshes and sandy heaths. The main distinction is its shorter legs and a capacity to run rather than walk or hop.

It's easy to see why, with the life cycle of frogs and toads undergoing dramatic physical transformations, many traditional cultures revered frogs and toads as beings with special or mysterious qualities. Many species also shed their skins regularly as they grow, and some species even eat the shed skin. It's not surprising they were given a symbolic significance around the world, along the themes of rebirth, fertility and transformation. How many of our familiar fairy tales involve being turned into, or back from, frogs and toads?

There is an impossibly rich font of folklore and superstition, particularly about toads, which were often portrayed as evil spirits or a witch's familiar. In *As You Like It*, Shakespeare's Old Duke testifies to 'the toad, ugly and venomous,' who 'wears yet a precious jewel in his head.' This was a bizarre but popular superstition of a 'toadstone' in the head of a toad, which, if worn as a protective charm, would apparently tell the wearer about the presence of poison by changing colour, or temperature. Who knew...?

Of our three native species of newt, the largest is the most distinctive and also the rarest. The handsome **great-crested newt** is up to 6 inches in length, and is coloured yellow-orange on its underside and a dark purple-brown above the belly. The high, denticulated crest of the male during the breeding season makes it easier to distinguish whereas the **palmate newt** and **smooth newt** are lookalikes, with the former having webbed hind feet.

Like our other amphibians, the best time to look for newts is in and around ponds during the breeding season in the early spring. In particular, watch how a male newt chases the female and then postures in front of her whilst vibrating his tail. The female then lays about 300 eggs, lovingly wrapping each one up in pondweed. These then hatch into newtpoles which will remain newt-like as they mature, assuming they escape predation of course.

ANIMAL THEATRE

Divide everyone into groups of four to six people. Ask each group to secretly decide upon one nocturnal creature that they will collectively embody. After a brief rehearsal period, the groups take turns to present their animal's movements and sounds to the others.

It's important to describe clearly what it means to embody an animal collaboratively. Explain that all the participants in each group will actively partici-

Equipment required:
None
Ages: 6 and up
Number of participants:
12–30

pate in creating a sculpture of one creature's body, and then they will also attempt to portray the animal's movement as accurately as possible. If the creature has a voice or makes a sound, they should include that in the presentation, too. Encourage the audience to refrain from guessing until the presentation is complete to give it proper air-time. Remember to applaud the performance!

DEATH BOX (AKA NATURE MUSEUM)

I know, it sounds a bit unsavoury, but this box of natural treasures never fails to disappoint. The box contains the residue and remains of creatures that have either passed on or passed by, such as feathers, skulls, bones, feet, wings, skins and exoskeletons. It's a collection that I've gathered over many years and which is useful stimulus for some natural history. Before a nightwalk, I like to bring out a few intriguing items from the nightwalk bag to enrich and inform and add texture to the experience.

People love props. We are a tactile species. We just love to touch and feel, smell and see close up the parts of animals and birds that are usually so elusive. Passing a tawny owl's wing or foot around the circle inevitably heightens interest. Pulling out the desiccated body of a long-eared bat is a striking way to introduce some of its fascinating features and characteristics. It's true that for the young and unacquainted, the first audible response can be, 'Euuurgh!' But this will often mature into a, 'Wow!' as the mystery and magic of nature's design concepts are revealed in myriad forms.

> **Equipment required:**
> 1 interesting or unusual box
> (please, no plastic bags!)
> Some dead things...
> **Ages:** 6 and up
> **Number of participants:**
> 2–30

I often use props such as skulls or skins to introduce nocturnal creatures like the badger and fox, or even moles, to an audience that has little experience with wild animals. A productive routine is to ask the group, 'What are your questions?' as they pass an object around the circle.

Remember though, in order to answer such questions and generally to lead this activity effectively, you'll have to do some homework to learn about the distinguishing features of anatomical structures like a badger skull or an owl feather. I've included some tracking books that are good sources of such information in the Links and Resources section on page 197.

CHAPTER 5

Learning the Night Sky

I have loved the stars too truly to be fearful of the night.
SARAH WILLIAMS, *Twilight Hours*

'I spin beneath my pyramid of night,' declared Percy Bysshe Shelley in *Prometheus Unbound*, introducing another confluence of the lyrical and the literal. For it is indeed true that the Earth wears a 'nightcap' whilst the Sun is on the other side, and the resulting darkness can be imagined like a pyramid or a Harry Potter wizard's hat rising to an apex. This is the Earth's shadow, with a diameter of 8,000 miles at the base, reaching 870,000 miles to its 'tip' in outer space, which makes for a nice round number of approximately 100 times taller than its diameter.

It's paradoxical, but you can see farther in the dark than you can during the day and this is made obvious under the night sky. When we gaze up at the stars we are looking at celestial objects impossibly far away, a view that hasn't really changed for millions of years. Modern science has extended our gaze further out into the great beyond, but when we behold with unaided eyes it's the same view and experience as our Neanderthal ancestors would have had.

For our ancestors the night sky was a calendar, clock and compass to orientate themselves. Certain constellations only appear at certain times of the year. The nomadic Bedouin people knew, for example, to sow their crops when the Pleiades star cluster appeared, and we can learn from our ancestors that when the constellation of Taurus the bull races ahead of the sunrise, the spring blossoms will shortly follow.

Ancient humans also reached up into this realm to draw down meaning and to help them make sense of the phenomenal world. The stories they projected onto the patterns of the stars are left behind for us to enjoy, as are the terms and frames of reference for celestial bodies still used in our contemporary language. The ancients saw the whole firmament as a stage, and in its constant motion, charted the dramatic entrances and exits, deaths and rebirths of its players. The stars, moon and planets were the vocabulary of the sky, and by characterising them as gods, heroes and animals, humans added a dimension of meaning to their lives.

For a simple form of connection to our ancestors, all we need do is step out at night and behold the same phenomena as they did, and feel the same things that they would have felt by gazing upward and outward. After all, you can't help but experience that profound sense of perspective that a starry sky invites. The big questions bubble up, as they must have done for our distant relatives too. Questions like, 'why are we here?', 'where do we come from?', 'what does it all mean?'.

Today we are somewhat blinded by the light, both symbolically and literally. More often than not, our beholding of the stars is polluted by the scourge of street lighting that brightens villages, towns and cities. But, when you can get far enough away, or if you are fortunate to travel in the desert or far out to sea, then you can enjoy a rare luxury in what activist and author Satish Kumar calls the 'million-star hotel'.

Astronomy is a vast subject, but a cursory visit to various celestial landmarks and phenomena it will suffice to equip you with enough basic knowledge to guide others on a wondrous journey through the night sky. It doesn't take much to engender that delicious sense of awe and wonder, and this chapter presents a combination of activities, facts and stories that can be served up during a feast of stargazing.

Astronomical Perspectives Explained

When I was a kid, nobody ever explained to me our place in the totality of space, or offered a perspective on the great cosmic dance of the galaxies. Looking back, that's an astonishing omission in my education, which, I'm sorry to say, wasn't filled with traditional narratives either, as our ancestors would have enjoyed. Traditional stories about the stars,

sun and moon were a way to engage with these observable but mysterious phenomena, and were full of meaning and implication, however
far-fetched. (And these stories from our solar system are the ultimately
far-fetched ones!)

An in-depth explanation is beyond the scope of this book, but here's a
simple version of what is happening all around our planet...

The Earth makes a complete turn on its axis, west to east, every
twenty-four hours. The stars seemingly remain as fixed points in space
all around us, which gives the impression that the sun, moon and our
neighbouring planets move from east to west, with some making one
full trip around the Earth each day. For example, at the onset of winter
and for a period of a few months, the constellation Orion rises in the
east and sets in the west about twelve hours later. You can watch it
make its progress, moving across the sky at 15 degrees (approximately
one fist held up to the night sky is 10 degrees) an hour. In a time span
of twenty-four hours, Orion will have passed overhead, set in the west
and then passed around the Earth, to rise again in the east. This is the
great illusion, that the stars are moving across our sky, and historically
nobody had reason to challenge this, until Copernicus published hereti-
cal theories which in a cultural, metaphorical and scientific sense turned
the world upside down. The Earth was spinning around the sun, not the
other way around. That was headline-grabbing news. Later discoveries
in astronomy revealed the movement through space of both stars and
whole galaxies, and now we know, despite appearances, everything is in
constant motion.

In addition to our daily spin around our own planet's axis, we are making an annual pilgrimage around the sun. We are orbiting in an easterly
direction, which makes the stars appear to 'travel' each night towards the
west at about 1 degree per day. Therefore, in six months' time, our night
sky will be filled with different stars.

If someone had explained all that to me when I was young and full
of curiosity about the world, I can't help but feel it might have helped
...somehow.

What follows are several activities you can draw upon to supplement
and deepen the experience of the night, accompanied by some key information about our cosmos.

About the Sun

Although this is a book about the dark, it doesn't feel right to leave out the beating heart from the body of the solar system. It is, after all, an off-stage presence at night, lighting up the face of the moon. Here, then, are some essential facts.

The sun's diameter is 109 times the size of Earth's and is one big ball of energy, made up of 90 per cent hydrogen, 9 per cent helium, and 1 per cent of all other elements. The main process at the core of the sun is a thermonuclear conversion of hydrogen into helium which is predicted to last another 7 billion years. Eventually, it will run out of fuel, ushering in its next phase. Our sun will then grow to become an enormous red giant, devouring Mercury, Venus and possibly Earth too in its path to self destruction.

Despite these impressive credentials, our sun is still a pretty unremarkable star compared to some of the extremes found elsewhere in our own galaxy and beyond.

From our knowledge about planetary orbits around the sun, you may presume that the sun is a stationary object. But the truth is the sun, along with the whole solar system, is moving along at what seems a fairly hectic pace. The entire system is revolving around the centre of the Milky Way in a huge orbit, which means, that at about 500,000 miles per hour, it takes around 225–250 million years for each orbit around the galaxy.

To quote Douglas Adams in *The Hitch-Hikers Guide to the Galaxy*, 'You may think it's a long way to the chemist, but that's just peanuts to Space.'

About the Moon

The birth of the moon in astronomical terms is an epic beginning. According to the 'Big Whack' theory (properly called the giant-impact hypothesis), the moon was formed from the debris that coalesced following a colossal impact between the Earth and another planetesimal. Although there are competing explanations, most astronomers concur that this is the most plausible genesis of the moon.

Although nearly 240,000 miles away, the moon is nevertheless our most accessible celestial body, our night-time guide and an ally for our ancestors in forming our concept of time.

The sun gives us the framework to chart the expanse of a single day, whereas the moon's repeated phases are suggestive of a cycle of birth, death and rebirth, and afford a way to understand longer patterns in the passage of time. Its dual aspect of constancy and change gave humanity an orientation to the unfolding of each day, month and year. The moon's cycle has dominion over earthly rhythms, such as the tides, and its other-worldly appearance and disappearance yielded the inspiration for beliefs, stories, rituals and thanksgiving throughout the ages amongst all peoples worldwide.

> *Sing, Muses, with your sweet voices,*
> *Sing, daughters of Zeus, son of Kronos,*
> *Sing us the story of the long-winged Moon.*   **HOMER**

Annually published almanacs contain information about cosmic cycles and tides, and were, in a very practical way, second in importance only to the Bible in olden times. Knowledge of the lunar cycle was helpful to travellers and farmers, and also benefitted smugglers to aid discreet navigation. Field labourers for example, knew they could take advantage of the moon in September because it rises almost as soon as the sun sets, which meant there was more time for harvesting. As the old adage goes: 'The moon of September shortens the night, the moon of October is the hunter's delight.'

For many ancient humans, the year's notation was a lunar one, taking 354 days. But, twelve moons cycles doesn't quite fit into our solar year, being short by eleven days. In AD 45. Julius Caesar extended that year to 445 days so that the new solar calendar of 365 days could begin the following year, with an extra day every four years to account for a minor discrepancy, giving us our leap year.

Despite the effect of the moon upon the tides, there is no real evidence that the gravitational pull of the moon affects people's behaviour. However, the imagined effects of the full moon are documented in our recent histori-cal past. In the fifteenth through seventeenth centuries, it was believed that women were 'particularly vulnerable' to the influence of the Moon – some twenty-two victims recorded in London in St Botolph's parish, dying 'suddenly of the moons effect', as described by A. Roger Ekirch in *At Day's*

Close. Moonstruck indeed. Cultures all over the world were fascinated with the shape-shifting curse upon humanity that some believed was brought on by the full moon. Most notably, in all those superstitions and stories of the werewolf.

Another effect of the Earth's celestial dancing partner has been the slowing of the Earth's rotation. Modern astronomers have proved the Earth used to spin much faster than it does now, so it turns out we can thank the moon for sparing us dizzy spells! The Earth spins more slowly because of the proximity of the Moon. How about that? I can equate this with the general 'vibe' of the night – everything being quieter, slower and still. The moon sailing solo across a seemingly empty sky also indulges our empathy with the moon for those times we also spend in solitude, feeling alone ourselves.

For the purposes of planning a nightwalk, it's worth getting acquainted with the patterns of the lunar month. That way you can, if you wish, find the best times to behold a moonrise or moonset. An almanac will provide you with the information you need or, of course, it can easily be found online. The gist of it is that the moon does the same 'dance' in one month as the sun does in one year, and so will rise on the easterly horizon at different points during the day or night.

For a peak experience of beholding the moon, when a telescope is not practical or available, I recommend using binoculars; the view they provide of details of the moon's surface is still amazing. Anyone who has never viewed the moon through a lens is in for a treat.

A note worth remembering is that for better views of the contours, craters and scars on the moon's surface, the best times are during the waxing and waning crescent phases, when the shadows are longer and more detail is revealed.

For me one of the most delicious experiences is to witness the rising of the full moon over the eastern horizon and provides a perfect focus for a group's silent attention (see Viewing Party on page 127). Depending on the topography of where you live, this may involve climbing a hill to gain an advantage point. The moment when a rising and reddish moon ascends the eastern horizon is breathtaking and will not fail to leave the group awestruck.

VIEWING PARTY

The Viewing Party is an idea adapted from the delightful and mindful Japanese custom of going out to collectively behold the cherry blossoms in the springtime by sitting under a cherry tree and drinking plum wine.

I encourage you to do something similar with the opportunity of a clear sky to behold the moon as it rises over the horizon. Do not underestimate the impact of this simple activity – if conditions are favourable it will engender awe and wonder, lending a dimension of the sacred to everyday life.

Equipment required:
Sit mats
Candle lantern
Refreshment basket
Ages: 8 and up
Number of participants:
4-16

Plan your viewing party on or around a full moon. On the evening of the actual full moon, the moon will be rising just as the sun is setting in a beautiful natural symmetry. (Every subsequent evening, or sometimes day the moon will rise approximately fifty minutes later, depending on the time of year.) The winter months are better for viewing parties because the sky turns dark early, bringing out the greatest detail in the moon as it makes its dramatic entrance onto the dusky stage.

If you don't live in a spot where you can see the horizon, remember that the moon rises in the eastern horizon, dances across the night sky 'chasing' the trail of the sun, and sets in the western horizon. There is some variation throughout the year so be sure to seek out a viewing platform that has a wide-angle perspective.

Make sure you consult the weather forecast in advance, as a Viewing Party without a view of the moon would be a different sort of party...

Prepare some appropriate refreshments, such as hot drinks if it's a cold night. Work out the schedule of the event carefully in advance, identifying the timing of the moon eclipsing the horizon and then allowing sufficient time to get in position nice and early. For most groups, no more than 20 minutes of quiet reflection in advance of moonrise is best, but a mature group might enjoy an even longer reflective time.

If you are facilitating a group experience as opposed to, say, sitting with a friend, I suggest a few further refinements to this experience to sweeten the proceedings.

Explain the event process so that everyone has a sense of what to expect, such as how far they will be walking and how long they will be sitting out in the night air.

On arriving at the 'viewing platform' start with some sort of attunement such as a discussion about the lunar cycle and the role of the moon in human cultures. Be creative! This could also be done using poetry (always better recited than read) or riddles, or even by telling a traditional narrative about the moon (refer to chapter 7 for suggestions of poems, riddles and stories).

Then invite everyone to take a sit mat and space out facing the horizon for some reflective time alone whilst they wait for the moonrise. Suggest everyone stay in range so that you can see them, because part of the richness of this experience is the sense of collective sharing. In this way, the activity has a different quality to it than a solo sit-spot (see page 44).

I often keep the refreshments a surprise, but that's not essential. After everyone has settled into position, before or after the moon's entrance, (not during), carry the mysterious basket of refreshments around to each individual to quietly administer their 'nocturnal medicine'.

Another lovely detail is to signal the time for the group to return to civilisation by lighting a candle lantern, which you can then use to guide the group back through the darkness (unless the terrain is so rough that stronger torchlight is needed for safe walking). Consider asking them to gather and walk back in silence, which can add to the reverential atmosphere. Some sharing can then take place if desired back at the campfire or meeting point. Or better still, wait until the morning after, if you have that possibility.

Notes and Variants
Sometimes things just don't work out to view a rising of the full moon – it might not be the right time of the month or the weather may not cooperate. Keep your options open; on a moonless night, conditions might be perfect for stargazing instead. You can choose to 'behold' anything – it's entirely your call where you want to place everyone's attention. It could

be, for example, to sit under an open sky, present to the incoming tide of darkness, and the first stars emerging

About the Planets

The information gathered from NASA space probes journeying far out into our solar system over the last few decades offers the most extraordinary up-to-date insights into the history and composition of the planets. In times past, they were seen as the dramatic players on the cosmic stage, moving capriciously amongst the fixed backdrop of stars. The planets are the nomads of the night sky and the Greek word *planētēs* means 'wanderers'.

During a nightwalk, even with the unaided eye we can view the cosmic dance of the nearer planets, and these are worth getting to know.

Venus

Venus is one of the easiest celestial bodies to perceive, shining especially brightly either just as the sun is setting low in the western sky, or before the sunrise in the eastern sky. Thus it's called the morning or evening star, and is clearly bigger and brighter than other stars. In fact, it's the third brightest object in the sky and it was consequently given the name of the Roman goddess of beauty and love. Venus is sometimes called our sister planet because of its proximity and similar size to Earth. But, whereas the various cosmic forces have made the Earth an optimal planet for life to flourish, Venus would fit very well with our notions of hell. It's devilishly hot on the surface, and it's heavily wrapped with toxic clouds of carbon dioxide and sulphuric acid, the density of which causes the atmospheric pressure at the surface to be about ninety times what it is on Earth. These clouds reflect at least 70 per cent of the sunlight it receives, which is what makes it shine so brilliantly at dawn and dusk.

Mars

More than any other visible planet, Mars fluctuates in its appearances in our night sky, being brighter and fainter in alternate years. Its variable brightness is one reason the ancient astronomers attributed war-like qualities to Mars, characterising these as the mood swings of a volatile war god, at times resting, at others on the war path.

We can discern Mars quite easily in the night sky with the naked eye. Its red colouration is due to the presence of iron oxide in its surface. However, it wasn't always a dry, cold and rocky planet. Data from space probes that have landed on Mars show it once had copious amounts of water and would then have been seen as a blue planet.

Mars has two moons, Phobos and Deimos, named after twin sons of Ares, the Greek god of war, who inspired the Roman god Mars. As an interesting side note, the author Jonathan Swift wrote about these 'two lesser stars' in *Gulliver's Travels*, probably influenced by the speculations of the astronomer Kepler. Strangely, however, these two moons were not discovered until 151 years *after* the book was written.

Jupiter

The undisputed ruler of our celestial kingdom is the vast gas giant Jupiter, the fourth brightest celestial object in the sky. Astronomers have recently understood more about the pivotal role it played in the formation of the solar system, and the crucial role it still plays. Its reputation as sovereign is, it turns out, well deserved. A simplified version of a more complex theory is that as Jupiter hurtled through its first orbit with its immense gravitational effect, it cleared a path, flinging all the space dust and debris far out into the asteroid belt, beyond Mars. However, more recently, astronomers have understood Jupiter to be more of a Jekyll and Hyde, with a more destructive role to play in Earth's future with its potential to 'sling-shot' the occasional asteroid or comet our way. That said, there's no harm in sending a little gratitude towards Jupiter whenever you see it, for the protection it does mostly afford us.

The planet's diameter is a whopping 88,695 miles and its mass equates to that of all the other solar system's planets, asteroids and satellites put together. Yet it's a bit of an optical illusion, albeit an enormous one, as it has no solid surface. Its upper atmosphere is in constant turmoil, which makes for ever-changing, stunningly beautiful patterns of streaming clouds, made up mainly of hydrogen and helium. It takes a powerful telescope to reveal these clouds, but the thrilling sight of Jupiter's four largest moons can be seen through a regular pair of binoculars. What speculating astronomers suggest is there might be as many as 600 moons orbiting Jupiter in total.

Saturn

The sixth planet from the sun is another huge gas giant: Saturn, the glittering jewel in the solar system's crown, with its magnificent ring system. To give you some perspective on its size, Saturn's rings, together with the planet itself, could fill the entire distance between the Earth and the moon.

Even though its relative size is great, Saturn's density is far less than Jupiter's. In fact, it has a density less than the density of water, which means if you could find a body of water large enough, Saturn would float!

Saturn is so far out it takes a lengthy twenty-nine and a half years to complete one orbit of the sun and its light takes approximately seventy-nine minutes to reach us.

Saturn's role in our story is no less significant than Jupiter's. As Jupiter went on the rampage through the solar system, creating havoc with its gravitational effect on everything in its path, Saturn arrived to save the day. Thanks to Saturn's own gravitational field, its own initial orbit and proximity to Jupiter effectively reigned in the giant planet and 'pulled' it back, so sparing Earth from its destructive force.

The Cassini space probe orbiting around Saturn has discovered many more moons, eighty two confirmed (but not all named) so far. The largest of these is Titan, the second biggest moon in the solar system after Jupiter's moon Ganymede. Titan is larger than the planet Mercury. If you view Saturn through binoculars, you can just barely see Titan as well. Intriguingly, along with several of Saturn's moons, Titan has an internal ocean that could feasibly hold microbial life.

Thanks to the space probe, we now know that Saturn's rings are made up of ice and rocks, a mere 10 metres (35 feet) thick in parts, which is why they can 'disappear' when viewed from certain angles. The rings extend outwards up to 175,000 miles from the planet. Somewhat poignantly, it is predicted that Saturn will lose its beautiful rings completely...in about 100 million years.

About the Constellations

Anyone who loved doing dot-to-dot pictures will love playing the same game with the constellations of the night sky. It's a bit more challenging of course, because there are no start and finish points, and you are not guided by a numbered sequence.

The magic here is in another confluence, one where myth meets maths. It was the storytellers who gave the constellations their image and identity, which in turn fed our collective imagination and interest in celestial matters. Because the sky was seen as the domain of the divine, it's not surprising that traditional cultures the world over painted scenes and images from their gods into the constellations. For our 'map of the skies' we have the Ancient Greeks, the Romans and the advanced cultures from the Middle East to thank for the stories and impressions they left behind.

Ptolemy, who was an Egyptian astronomer of Greek descent during the second century AD, was not the originator of the tales, but his contribution was a masterpiece of curation and projection onto the night sky screen, imagining forty-eight constellations into being. His treatise on astronomy still influences the way we gaze up at the stars today.

Needless to say, there were competing narratives from successive and other cultures, and, together with modern developments in astronomy, a more definitive map from a global perspective was created for a contemporary and scientific world. In 1922 the International Astronomical Union set about clearing up the confusion, and by 1930 they had charted and formalised eighty-eight constellations on a basis of international agreement (half of these were created and documented by Ptolemy). Although the science is now the dominant lens through which we look at the stars, the rich brew of narrative projections onto the ultimate blank (and black) canvas is the most profound and healthy 'screen time' you will ever wish to have.

Zodiac constellations are those that lie along the plane of the ecliptic, which is the apparent path of the sun across the sky, as seen from Earth. In other words, the sun appears, to us, to pass through these constellations over the course of a year. It's also a variable pattern from year to year. The passage of the sun through the zodiac is a cycle that ancient cultures used to determine the cosmic influences, and to predict weather patterns and growth cycles.

Today, the term zodiac, which comes from the Greek, translating literally as the 'ring of animals', is mostly associated with astrology, with the twelve signs of the western zodiac corresponding to the twelve constellations seen along the ecliptic. The so-called cardinal signs Aries, Cancer, Libra and Capricorn mark the beginning of the four seasons. The sun is said to enter these signs on the first days of spring, summer, autumn and winter, respectively.

When to See the Constellations

Here's a summary of the times of year when the major constellations are visible in northern night skies.

All year: Cassiopeia, Cepheus, Draco, Camelopardalis, Ursa Major and Ursa Minor
Spring: Leo, Boötes, Virgo, Corvus, Crater, Cancer and Hydra
Summer: Aquila, Cygnus, Lyra, Hercules, Sagittarius, Scorpius and Ophiuchus
Autumn: Pegasus, Andromeda, Perseus, Triangulum, Aquarius, Capricornus and Pisces
Winter: Taurus, Canis Major, Canis Minor, Gemini, Orion, Auriga, Perseus, Cetus and Eridanus

A full accounting of the lore of the constellations would fill a book of its own. Here is just a taste of star lore. To learn more, refer to some of the excellent sources listed in the Bibliography on page 199.

Andromeda is the nearest and brightest of all the spiral galaxies we can perceive, lying a mere 2.5 million light years beyond the Milky Way. In Greek mythology, Andromeda was the daughter of Queen **Cassiopeia**, and in that story, the sea god Poseidon was so angered by her mother's vain boasting he sent the sea monster Cetus to ravage their kingdom. The innocent Andromeda was offered as sacrifice and chained to a rock before being saved by Perseus. Set into the sky by Poseidon, Cassiopeia spends six months every year upside down to atone for her vanity.

Aquarius is often connected to Ganymede, the cup-carrier to the Olympian gods. In Greek mythology, Zeus became so infatuated with this beautiful son of King Tros that he shape-shifted into an eagle in order to carry the boy off to Olympus.

Aries was the winged ram with a golden fleece that was sent by the nymph Nephele to rescue the two children of King Athamas, and whose fleece became the prize sought by Jason and the Argonauts.

A Greek Story of Orion

This story includes the story of several constellations: Orion, Lepus, Taurus and Sagittarius.

Once upon a time, Zeus, the mighty king of the gods, was travelling through the countryside, along with his brothers Poseidon and Mercury. It was getting late, and they were far from any comfort, so they disguised themselves and stopped for the night at a shepherd's house. Not realising the identity of his guests, the old shepherd offered what hospitality he could, and sacrificed and cooked his last cow for their dinner. The gods were impressed by the old man's generosity and asked him what he desired most in the world. The old shepherd replied that he wished he could have had a son. With a blinding flash of light, Zeus, Poseidon and Mercury revealed themselves and promised to fulfil the old shepherd's wish.

The gods gathered around the hide of the cow that they had just eaten, performed a mystical ceremony and bundled up the cow skin. They told the old man to wait for three moons before undoing the bundle. A few months' later, the old man, with trembling hands, untied the bundle to see a beautiful baby boy lying inside. He was overjoyed and named the boy **Orion**.

As Orion grew he became a great hunter. As a young man, he came across the seven sisters of the Pleiades and with all his ardour he pursued them relentlessly until Zeus had to lift them into the sky out of reach of his unrequited affections. Orion's reputation as a skilled hunter grew, and before long came to the attention of Artemis, goddess of the hunt, who became his lover.

The god Apollo (brother of Artemis), became jealous of Orion and killed him with a scorpion. In her sorrow Artemis begged Zeus to place him in the sky amongst the most brilliant stars, where he could remain for all eternity with his hunting dogs **Canis Major** and **Canis Minor**, chasing the hare **Lepus**. So

Zeus honoured Orion in this way, depicting him as facing the snorting charge of **Taurus** the bull, whose red eye is the star Aldebaran. Afterwards, Apollo insisted that the scorpion also be placed in the sky to commemorate the great hunter's downfall. Zeus agreed, but placed **Scorpius** the scorpion on the opposite side of the sky so as one rises, the other always sets. Zeus also placed **Sagittarius** the archer next to the scorpion, with drawn bow aimed at the scorpion's heart, should the scorpion try to advance towards Orion and sting him again.

The Orion constellation is one of the most familiar, hunting in our night sky from east to west between early autumn and late spring. Because it stands above the equator, it is visible to every inhabited place on Earth.

Cancer is the crab, Karkinos that Hercules, during a fight with the many-headed monster Hydra, booted into the sky. Fittingly, for such a minor role the crab became one of the fainter constellations in the zodiac.

Canis Major's constellation contains Sirius, also known as the dog star, which is the brightest star in our sky. Curiously, it has taken various forms of a canine in many diverse traditional cultures: a wolf, fox or jackal, and in Greek mythology, it is a large dog following at the heels of the mythical hunter Orion in pursuit of a hare, which is represented by the constellation Lepus. In one version of the story, the dog, Laelaps, famed for always catching whatever it hunted, was put on the trail of the Teumessian fox, which it was said could never be caught. Out of pity, Zeus intervened in their fate and placed them in the sky where they continue to play out the eternal hunt with the fugitive fox, **Canis Minor**, rising in the sky an hour or so before Canis Major, the hunting dog.

Their annual emergence was timed with the hottest time of the year in the Mediterranean; the Greeks and Romans both recognised the stifling 'dog days'.

Closer observations in the modern era also revealed that the 'dog' had a 'pup', a companion or binary star, now called Sirius B, which helps explain its brightness. Another reason for it brightness is that it's only a relative astronomical stone's throw away, at just over 8.6 light years distance.

You can find Sirius by first locating Orion's belt, and then following an imaginary line continuing straight down. We tend to see it in the late winter evening skies and the pre-dawn skies of late summer.

Capricornus derives from a Sumerian/Babylonian amphibious 'sea goat' but the Greeks associated this constellation with their forest deity, Pan, who had the horns and legs of a goat.

Cassiopeia (see Andromeda)

Corona Borealis or the 'northern crown' is a small ring of stars, near the red giant star Arcturus, known in Greek times as the 'crown of Ariadne'. In that legend, Ariadne saved Theseus from the Minotaur, married the god Dionysus, and wore a jewelled crown at their wedding, made by Hephaestus the god of fire.

Gemini was named after the mythical twin half-bothers Castor and Pollux, who became the patron saints of Greek sailors. Their heads are denoted by two of the constellation's brightest stars.

Hercules was based on the Greek god Heracles, but even they lost the origins of this constellation. As befits their greatest hero, whom they depicted in the sky as 'the kneeling one', the stories are long and complex.

Leo is connected to the Nemean lion, killed by Heracles as one of his Twelve Labours. After his arrows failed to penetrate the lion's skin, he vanquished the ferocious beast by choking it and then wore its pelt as a cloak.

Libra is the only inanimate object represented in the zodiac and means 'balance' or 'scales' in Latin. To the Romans, it was a favoured constellation as they believed Rome was founded when the moon was in Libra.

Pisces is linked to the goddess Aphrodite and her son Eros who were pursued by a hundred-headed monster called Typhon. They leapt into the river Euphrates and were carried to safety on the backs of two fish.

Ursa Major is perhaps the most familiar constellation and means 'great bear' in Latin. It is associated with myths in many cultures and represents a bear in many legends, particularly in the northern hemisphere. It's also known as the Plough in the UK, the Big Dipper in the US and the Saucepan in France. Its seven stars variously represent seven sages or seven blacksmiths,

Ursa Major and Minor: A Bears' Tale

Long ago, in the time where the Greek gods lived on Mount Olympus and ruled over the people, there was a beautiful daughter of a king of Arcadia who was called Callisto. One day, the king of all the gods, Zeus, noticed her accompanying Artemis, the goddess of the hunt. Zeus fell in love and seduced her and then tried to keep his affair with Callisto hidden from his wife, the goddess Hera.

But, in time, Callisto gave birth to Zeus' son Arcas, and soon Hera learnt of what had transpired. As a punishment, the jealous Hera turned Callisto into a bear and banished her to roam in the wild country. Over the years, Arcas grew into a great hunter. One day, whilst hunting far into the woods, he came upon a bear, and was amazed that it didn't turn and run from him. Unknown to Arcas, this bear was his own mother Callisto. Callisto recognised her grown son, and was filled with a desire to speak with him but she could only growl. Seeing the bear advance on him, Arcas grabbed his spear and drew his sword. And there would surely have been a tragic outcome had not Zeus intervened. To protect them both, he changed Arcas into a bear as well. As a rebuff to Hera, and to keep them from further harm, Zeus placed both of the bears high up in the sky out of Hera's reach, but within her sight every night of the year. It is said that the bears' tails are longer than normal because Zeus grabbed them both by their tails and whirled them around his head, stretching their tails, and then flung them upward.

But in this story of the gods, Hera gets the last word by forbidding the bears from ever resting beneath the Earth, and that is why they can never set below the horizon.

or in one myth the seven brothers that stole away one of the seven sisters in the Pleiades, which is one 'explanation' for why we now only see six stars in that constellation. The two front stars are known as the Pointers, as an imaginary line extending from them always leads to Polaris, the Pole Star, or North Star. This easily discerned pattern of motion, wheeling around the fixed Pole Star helped people track time both through the night and the seasonal calendar.

The second star of the 'pan's handle' has a fainter star called Alcor, which is just visible, and was used as an eyesight test for the Arab sailors in olden times – if you could see it, you could sail.

Ursa Minor mirrors the shape of Ursa Major and although much smaller, is nevertheless a significant constellation for its position in the night sky, and for containing the Pole Star, located at the tip of the 'pan's handle'.

Virgo is the largest constellation and connected to Dike, the Greek goddess of justice. Having experienced the Golden Age of mankind, she was dismayed by its decline, deciding in the end to abandon humanity to its fate, and reside in the heavens instead, in proximity to the constellation Libra.

Perseid Meteor Shower

In August every year, we are treated to a spectacular display of shooting stars. As the Earth orbits around the sun, it passes through the debris of a comet called Comet Swift-Tuttle. As particles enter Earth's atmosphere, friction causes them to burn up and we see the streak of light like a 'falling star'. Because of the angle of perception, it seems to be located in the constellation of Perseus, though they have no real connection otherwise. For the best viewing, the early hours of the morning are when the Earth turns to face the oncoming stream, the so-called 'children of Perseus'.

The Milky Way

It was Galileo peering through his telescope who enlightened the contemporary western world that the Milky Way was, in fact, made up of countless stars. The Milky Way can only be seen when viewed in a sufficiently dark sky, but when it is this luminous river of stars is a revelation. These days, 60 per cent of Europeans and 80 per cent of Americans now live where they cannot see this spectacle because of light pollution.

Bioluminescence

A wonderfully strange phenomenon that occurs in nature is **bioluminescence**, poetically known as 'foxfire' in old England. This greeny-bluish light found on rotting wood can be especially prevalent in moist, damp oak woods and will be easiest to spot on dark, moonless nights when you are lurking without a torch.

The strange light, also called 'fairy fire' or 'will-o-the-wisp', was considered something mystical. It wasn't until the nineteenth century that a scientific explanation arrived, revealing that this particular peculiar glow comes from the mycelial strands of fungus, as a result of a chemical reaction that occurs as the fungus breaks down the rotten wood. But, even though the mechanisms became understood, it's still a bit of a puzzle as to why the fungal organism glows. It's currently thought that the glow attracts insects that will bear the fungal spores away, increasing the likelihood of reproduction.

Sometimes, though, there's also an opportunity to be had in withholding rational explanation for phenomena. Instead, I like to fuel the fire of the imaginations of younger children by speculating with them about what the mysterious light might be. I believe this sort of creative process is a helpful part of endearing the natural world, and the mystery of life, to children.

Whatever the explanation given, or not given, it will always provide a nightwalk with a delightful pinch of magic.

In olden times, in Europe, the Milky Way was widely perceived as a celestial road, but to the ancient Arabs it was referred to as the *darb al-tabbāna*, or 'hay merchants way'. The indigenous Australians saw it differently again, as a celestial river. To the Bushman, however, it was campfire ashes, and to the ancient Egyptians it was wheat spread by the goddess Isis. Needless to say, these perceptions fed cosmology and traditional narratives. In a wonderful confluence of science and myth, we have discovered that this 'luminous river' is indeed a whirlpool and that at its core lurks a frightful 'monster' that devours everything in its path: a black hole, 'feeding' on stars that disappear into it's mysterious, ravenous 'belly'.

The Greek name for the Milky Way is derived from the Greek word for milk and also gives us our word galaxy. One legend from this tradition explains how the Milky Way was created. Zeus was fond of his son Heracles who was born of a mortal woman, and he decided to let the infant Heracles suckle on his divine wife Hera's milk when she was asleep, an act that would endow the baby with god-like qualities. When Hera awoke and realised that she was breastfeeding an unknown infant, she pushed him away and the spurting milk became the Milky Way.

In Irish mythology, the main name of the Milky Way was the 'Way of the White Cow'. It was regarded as a heavenly reflection of the sacred River Boyne, which is described as the Great Silver Yoke.

The Aurora Borealis

The aurora borealis is that eerie, shimmering night show that lights up the skies. For the most part, it is visible only rarely in the north of Scotland and the Scottish Isles, though, that being said, it has appeared as far south as Pembrokeshire in Wales. If you are fortunate to be in those areas of dark skies in the far north, just maybe you will be lucky to experience this other worldly event, that happens on average every few months.

There's no more dramatic experience of the sky than a full-blown aurora borealis. Not surprisingly, such phenomena records itself in the folklore of northern cultures. My favourite narrative, however, is from a Finnish folk tale that describes the fugitive Arctic fox's tail brushing the mountains of the north to produce sparks that become the northern lights.

These lights are a consequence of activity on the Sun. From explosions on the sun's surface, charged particles are catapulted into space and some of these will occasionally travel towards Earth. These are captured by Earth's magnetic field, acting like a protective shield and guided towards the polar region, where these particles collide with gas molecules in the atmosphere. The energy released from this collision gives off light and, depending on the molecular structure of the gas, this can result in a range of different colours – green, blue, yellow and even red.

Star Navigation

Another aspect of star lore is the orientation provided by the constellations for navigating at night. Our ancestors were not equipped with our modern GPS technology and so had to rely on their knowledge of the stars to travel at night. It's not that you will necessarily need the stars to navigate your way through the darkness on a nightwalk, but it nevertheless provides something of interest and enrichment during the nocturnal experience to allude to some orientation points.

A whole host of animals including birds, fish and even dung beetles have gazed upwards to plot their course on land and sea when daytime orientation was not possible. Humans, too, of course. The Vikings for example would use the Pole Star to navigate home following their punishing raids on Britain.

The most obvious orientation to north is drawn from Polaris, or the Pole Star, which, helpfully, is circumpolar (it never sets). If you can locate the the Plough, then you can draw an imaginary straight line by joining the two end stars and extending out in a straight line into a dark patch of sky; that is where it connects to Polaris.

The moon traces the path laid out by the sun, rising in the eastern sky and setting in the western sky. If there's a crescent moon, you can draw an imaginary straight line between the 'horns' down to the horizon. This will always give you a due south orientation.

Likewise, when the constellation of Orion is above you, you can locate the direction of due south by the direction his 'sword' is pointing.

In the summer, you can find a triangle shape traced between three stars: Vega, Deneb and Altair. When this 'summer triangle' is at its highest point in its rotation east to west, its lower star, Altair, points directly south.

STARGAZING

Some of the most exquisite outdoor experiences I have shared with a group have been on those rare warm summer nights in the UK, when the sky is clear and there is no moon to dilute the intensity of a confection of stars. Such a night is perfect for stargazing.

Equipment required:
Blankets
Candle lanterns
Ages: 8 and up
Number of participants:
2–25

The framework of a stargazing event is simple. Before the group arrives, spread out blankets on the ground in an open area and light several candle lanterns. That way, when you escort the group to the area, it's an unexpected and delightful discovery.

Invite your companions to lie down on the blankets and look up at the sky. I like to weave the theme of time travel into this activity, saying something like: 'Hey, night-watchers! Anyone up for some time travel? Just step into my time machine over here! All that's required is to lie down and gaze up at the stars. Plenty of room for everyone!'

Once everyone is comfortable, allow some minutes to pass so they can take in the view of the firmament.

One option is to simply allow people to enjoy the deep silence and reverence that this astonishing perspective affords. Or, you can offer a bit of narrative, which can be short or extensive, according to the variables of time, age, temperature and the extent of your knowledge of the night sky.

Here's how I might narrate a stargazing session:

'Now, don't forget to buckle up, we are going to go pretty fast! You might be feeling relaxed, but consider that this beautiful planet of ours is like a spaceship cruising through the solar system. The Earth travels at sixty thousand miles an hour, orbiting the sun. Hold on tight! Consider now that the surface of the Earth is spinning whilst it's orbiting, at a thousand miles an hour. That's how come we have day and night, turning towards and away from the light of the sun.

Nobody knows how many stars there are in the universe, but we do know that there are more stars than there are grains of sand in the world. Now that begins to give us an immediate perspective on the scale of the universe, especially when you think of how many sandy deserts and beaches there are. It would probably take you a week just to count the grains in one handful of sand.

On a clear, moonless night like tonight, we can see up to two and a half thousand stars with our unaided eyes. It's not many compared to the vast total, but think of each one as a different and unique world. That seems like it's a busy sky, but it's a bit of an optical illusion, when you consider how far apart the stars are. For example, apart from the Sun, which is our nearest star at 93 million miles away, the nearest star in the night sky visible to the naked eye is Alpha Centauri, which is nearly four and a half light years away. And that's just the nearest star. You can now begin to imagine the distances of the furthest visible stars, and they are only the ones that our probes can find as they travel out to research deep space, at the outer fringes of our solar system.

If you would like a really mind-bending concept, then consider that there are some stars so far out in the universe that their light has not yet arrived in our solar system.'

(At this point, I pause for a moment.)

'Choose one star now to focus on. Consider that this star may be so far away that even though you can still see its light, it might no longer exist. The distances are so great that whilst the light is still travelling, the star may well have reached the end of its existence. Or, perhaps when the light that you are seeing now first left the star, dinosaurs were roaming on Earth.

That's how stargazing is a form of time travel. The light you see twinkling in the sky left the star a very, very long time ago.

(Choose a star yourself and use it as an example; a star like Arcturus, which at thirty-seven light years away means the light you are seeing left its home in 1983.)

We are peering into the past...

This perspective makes it all the more remarkable that our planet has somehow contrived all the right conditions for life to flourish. Just enough oxygen, just enough carbon and hydrogen and nitrogen etc. It's really rather miraculous.'

＊ ＊ ＊ ＊ ＊ ＊ ＊ ＊ ＊

MAPPING CONSTELLATIONS

In this activity, the group works together to map out familiar constellations on the ground before trying to find them in the sky. It's a great way to help tell the stories of the constellations when it's not possible to do actual stargazing. This activity helps locate at least six constellations that are always visible in the northern hemisphere year-round; they constantly rotate around the Pole Star.

Equipment required:
White or light-coloured
  stones or chalks
Planispheres (optional)
Ages: 10 and up
Number of participants:
6–25

If you need a refresher on what some of the constellations look like, refer to the planisphere or the Resources section on page 197 for recommendations of star guides.

Choose a central point, such as a campfire if you've built one, which can represent the Pole Star in an imaginary night sky. From there, use the stones or chalks as the 'stars' in the constellations. Let the group do as much as they can on their own, but also step in to help if they are making mistakes or don't know the pattern of a particular constellation.

Start by asking the group to lay out the seven stars of the Plough (also called the Big Dipper and part of the constellation Ursa Major). If needed, remind them that the two pointers at the end of the 'plough' should line up in a straight line that points to the Pole Star.

Next, on the opposite side of the central point, place the five bright stars of Cassiopeia. Pick out some smaller stones to make the pattern of four fainter circumpolar constellations: the Little Dipper (part of Ursa Minor), King (Cepheus), Dragon (Draco) and Giraffe (Camelopardalis). These constellations may appear high or low in the sky, but in our latitude in the UK they can be seen any time of year.

Many constellations travel round the Pole Star once a day/night but at times they are hidden below the horizon. For example, Orion is pretty elusive in this month of May as he hides under the 'cloak' of daylight. Likewise the Pleiades, located on the end of one of the bull's horns in the Taurus constellation, is only clearly visible at night between October and March. It's worth consulting a planisphere to see what positions they are in the sky on the night you are observing.

After the group has mapped out the constellations on the ground, challenge them to move away from the central fire or light and see if they can locate the constellations in the sky. As they point out a constellation, you can share some fun facts and stories such as the tale of Orion's glittering sword – see About the Constellations on page 131 for more inspiration. With a few sessions like this, the constellations become part of the sky's furniture, and a helpful orientation in the hours of darkness.

Notes and Variants

If you want to do this activity on moonless nights, away from the campfire in the deeper dark of the forest, you could use electric tea lights or daub some glow-in-the-dark paint on the stones in advance so that the patterns will be easier to see.

CHAPTER 6

Leading Night-time Nature Outings

*To go in the dark with a light is to know the light.
To know the dark, go dark. Go without sight,
and find that the dark, too, blooms and sings,
and is traveled by dark feet and dark wings.*

WENDELL BERRY

N ever underestimate the apprehension that may accompany the prospect of setting out on a nightwalk; after all, it's such an unusual thing to do. Depending on the profile of your companions, they may well be full of trepidation or tingling with excitement at the prospect of venturing out into unchartered territory. It's as well to bear this in mind as you design your walk and consider the tone you wish to set at the beginning.

To illustrate: I have been fortunate to travel in some exotic locations and experience what it feels like to be outgunned by predators that would look upon me as a prospective meal. It's an unnerving, humbling, exciting experience to feel that kind of exposure and vulnerability, and it has an interesting effect on one's sensory awareness. Specifically, it ratchets up every cell and fibre of one's being to be present to the potential threats lurking everywhere. Quite frankly, I have never felt so alive.

It's this quality that can occasionally be introduced to a nightwalk experience – where appropriate, of course. It would not do to frighten youngsters and undo all the relationship-building work hitherto undertaken to acquaint everyone favourably with the night. But for those with the right sensibilities, before you begin a sit-spot or circle walk or fire stalk, it's a little bit of spice at night to introduce the possibility, that there might be something higher up the food chain out there...

For example, myths and legends abound when it comes to the suggestion of big cats abroad in Britain, and I can resonate with writer George Monbiot's perspective on the cultural longing for something wild and exciting, expressed through imaginary sightings. But I used to dismiss all reports of sightings of big cats in the UK – until recently.

I was told of a whole group who together saw a big cat in the forest here in Devon. When you have a group sighting as opposed to an individual's unsubstantiated account, it's time to pay more attention. I then began to seek out those who have supposedly witnessed big cats and I have had some interesting conversations, ranging from many far-fetched to the downright compelling. The sightings sometimes corroborated each other, and some people convinced me they had not imagined what they'd seen. But, even so, there still remained a doubt at the back of my mind. After all, surely there had to be some actual evidence of a body or scat or prints, or even a clear photograph?

And then, some colleagues of mine upcountry brought me some video footage caught on their motion-capture night vision camera they had set in the forests of Gloucestershire.

There's now no doubt in my mind that big cats do indeed operate in and around the margins of these lands, and many of you will have also heard of plausible sightings, as well as a larger number of spurious encounters.

I'm being quite playful with this suggestion to raise the idea with a group that there just might be big cats roaming in our forests. Timing is important and I suggest waiting until a group is acclimatised to the night, or perhaps when you work with a group that has even developed a complacency, which you perceive as an impediment to appreciating the night.

You can always qualify the mention of big cats with the rationale that even in their home territories, big cats rarely attack humans and that their priority is to avoid detection at all costs, at which they are very competent. There hasn't been an incident on these shores anyway, not since our last native (quite) big cat, the dear-departed Lynx, went extinct in about AD 700.

Whether you are subscribed to their presence in the British countryside or not, there is comfort in this being a near-impossible eventuality. But, even if it is only in our imagination, I reckon it's kind of good to 'feel' that threat, if only because it brings a sharpness to our awareness, and a bit of electricity to a night experience.

The very best timing to begin a nightwalk is during twilight in order to allow enough time for some 'attunement' before meeting the night.

Nightwalk Whats and Wherefores

The attunement process is important to set the tone for your nightwalk. Being outdoors as the light levels dwindle is helpful in terms of allowing our night vision to reach an optimal level. It's ideal to set out on the walk itself before the sky goes completely dark.

However, even if your timing is right, and even if the habitat is bursting with wildlife potential, be prepared to manage your companions' expectations of what might come into view. The profile of the group will be a determining factor; as I'm sure you will appreciate, there is a world of difference between a large contingent of excitable, apprehensive 10-year-olds and a small group of curious adults. To start with, spell out the impact of noise on nocturnal nature. Then, if leading a group of children, with assistance from any supporting adults who are part of the group, endeavour to manage the human noise output as best you can. It's probably unrealistic to expect some children to remain soundless throughout the walk. If they

Nightwalk Essentials List

First aid kit
Spare torch and batteries
Mobile phone for emergency services
Risk assessment
Toilet bag (containing toilet paper, hand gel, trowel)
Whistle or other communication device

are enjoying some of the activities and explorations, children will naturally vocalise. For such groups, I recommend relaxing some principles (like the importance of silent movement). Turn the valve and allow a little 'air pressure' to escape at times.

Even if you are unsuccessful in your attempts to cultivate a reverential atmosphere, because the kids are having so much fun that they can't contain their excitement, please remember that a nightwalk is still going to be a significant experience for them. Even though your hopes and expectations are not realised in the way you might have wanted, they will remember the night they ventured into the wild darkness for the rest of their lives.

If you find that you have an affinity for leading people on outdoor outings, there are a number of possible routes to qualify yourself as a guide, though none specifically for night walks. (Some mountain and moorland leadership courses include instruction on night navigation techniques with map and compass.) Basic principles of caretaking and good leadership in the outdoors can be learnt on a variety of short, affordable courses, and an outdoor first aid qualification is a bare minimum if you plan to lead a group outing with more than the members of your immediate family. Above all, you want to feel comfortable in your role, and to that end, here are a few basic tips on how to prepare for the role of nightwalk leader:

- Spend time outdoors in the dark on your own, to develop your own literacy with the night realm.
- Rehearse the route you will take with a group. Look for the stopping points, and for alternative access/exit points in case of a need to evacuate unexpectedly. Assume that some participants may not be sure-footed and ensure the route is easily navigable by a group in the dark. What can seem easy in the light of day may be much more challenging in the dark. Seek a route without impediments and obstacles. You might be able climb over a gate quickly, for example, but with a large group, getting everyone over the gate could cause considerable and unwelcome delay.
- Do a risk assessment to cover possible accident and injury scenarios.
- Make a list of everything you will need, including the items on the Nightwalk Essentials list, plus all the equipment for any activities or games you have planned as part of the outing.

- Keep the numbers small, ideally less than a dozen, particularly as you are learning the ropes.

On a cautionary note, it's as well to inform yourself about the presence of ticks in your region, and specifically in the area you are taking a group into. The incidence of Lyme disease associated with deer ticks is spreading fast in the UK; indeed it is three times more prevalent than it was ten years ago, and so do your research on how best to protect yourselves.

THE NIGHT-WATCHERS

Equipment required:
1 interesting-looking bag to carry everything
Pen torches
Yellow tape
Candle lantern
Matches
Charcoal
White sage
A5 size pre-written laminated cards with reflective strips
Blank postcards for sketching on
Owl-calling whistle
Ages: 9 and up
Number of participants: 8–16

In this delightful activity sequence, a mysterious 'Night-watcher' visits the group to guide them into the domain of the night-time.

The ideal setting of the Night-watcher's dramatic entrance is the campfire, with the group all sitting around in the early evening. The ideal timing for this is late twilight with dusk approaching, just before it is properly dark. Out of the twilight a mysterious cloaked figure suddenly appears with a candle lantern and a staff and a bag slung over his (or her) shoulder. 'Oh, its Jon,' says someone – but it's not 'Jon' as you normally see him. Apart from wearing a dark cloak, his face is smudged with charcoal and he smells of the herb sage. He then introduces himself as the Night-watcher, about to do his round, and he explains how his costume helps him fit in better to the night world. Then he continues:

'Have you noticed the way that for half the time, the Earth is in shadow? The way that day turns into night? How the birds quieten down and the atmosphere changes? Well, it's at this time that the Night-watchers start their rounds, checking that everything is as it should be. It would be great if I could show you what we do, because we need others to learn the secrets of my profession. Would anyone like to join me tonight?'

Of course they would! Excitement mounts at the prospect of a mysterious night excursion.

'OK then. I'm pleased to see you are wearing long sleeves, dark clothing and soft shoes for sneaking. It means the creatures out there will recognise us as Night-watchers and hopefully not be too disturbed. [If a group needs to change, this is when they would do that.] Before we leave, you'll also need something to disguise your face and mask your human smell.'

Charcoal sticks and sage are handed around the group, and the ritual of blackening faces and hands, and rubbing sage on clothing is followed before the Night-watcher issues a final instruction.

'Follow me as quietly as you can, and let's use only our night eyes to see with.'

By the light of a single lantern and the gentle light of a staff member's torch, the group follows a trail led by the Night-watcher into the woods.

Along the trail, the Night-watcher makes three or four stops that are discovered via the presence of a sign marked with reflective strips. Torches are handed out and the signs are read aloud, each an invitation to explore the night using different senses, for example:

- Listening to the sounds of the night
- Perceiving the shadows of the night by tracing with an index finger the outlines of the landscape and its features
- Underworld safari – using pen torches to explore patterns and features (similar to the Minibeast Safari activity on page 103)

The group then gathers to share their discoveries. Following this, they hand in the torches. The Night-watcher leads the group to a clearing, with a view to the night sky.

'To be a true Night-watcher, you must learn to travel alone, so you can learn that the night is beautiful and to be enjoyed. I invite you now to walk away to a spot on your own, where you can still see the lantern, as far as you dare. Then, sit down to experience being 'alone' in the peace of the night. I will blow out the candle, and when I light it again, after about ten minutes, make your way quietly back. Good luck everyone, and enjoy!'

On the way back to camp or the starting point, the last invitation is offered in a place with a clear view of the stars. The Night-watcher invites everyone to lie on their backs for some stargazing and when all are in position, the Night-watcher begins his narrative of our place in space. (See Stargazing activity narrative on page 142.)

And finally, just before the journey back to the starting point, the last words are spoken:

'OK everyone, my night rounds are complete. Thank you for joining me tonight. You now belong to our association of Night-watchers, and can do your own rounds anytime. You've learnt the main secret, that the shady side of sunship Earth is not as frightening as it may have seemed. Let's return to the campfire to enjoy some more of our sun's stored energy. Now it's time to practice some of the skills you've learnt. How about we travel in silence on the way back in case there are more of night's passengers to see or hear?'

Notes and Variants

From this description, you'll have realised that this activity requires a good amount of advance planning to gather materials and to write up the cards, affix the reflective strips and set out the cards along the trail.

Although this is a prescribed activity sequence from the Institute for Earth Education, you may vary the activities and adapt it to make it fit the time, setting and age group you are working with. Be aware that it won't then represent the Institute's recommended and precise protocols for Night-watchers as described in their programmes. It is, however, always good practice to acknowledge the source and inspiration of the activity, even if your version strays from the original.

Sample Nightwalks

Needless to say, there are endless flavours and combinations to make use of in designing an excursion into the dark and what follows are suggestions only. Feel free to curate your own programme of activity using these as a guideline to suit your requirements and experience. You'll see that each of these samples has a different theme with some clearly more suitable for older age groups. Use them as they are or as a starting point for planning a walk and then adapt them according to the profile of your group.

EXAMPLE 1 –
NATURALIST NIGHTWALK
Set the context: dusk as threshold
    time; recite a poem
Stealth games: Owls & Voles,
    Ring the Bell
Set the tone about nocturnal nature
Noses
Bat & Moth
Bat Detecting
Return to the campfire for a story

EXAMPLE 2 –
NATURALIST NIGHTWALK 2
Set the context: dusk as threshold
    time; recite Wendell Berry poem
Nocturnal Soundscape
Glow-worms
Owl Calling
Return for a story by the fire

EXAMPLE 3 –
STAR TREK (SEE PAGE 142)
Set the context: stargazing
Silent walk to a sky viewpoint
Lay down on blankets
Silent beholding
Star narrative
Star navigational aids
Return for a story by the fire

EXAMPLE 4 –
REVERENCE WALK
Set the context: why is it dark?
Nocturnal Soundscape
Silent walk
Recite David Whyte poem
    'Sweet Darkness'
Sit-spot
Return for a story by the fire

EXAMPLE 5 –
NIGHT-WATCHERS

Night-watcher's entrance
    to the fireside
Invitation to join the 'night rounds'
The Night Round (including
    Underworld Safari)
Return for a story by the fire

EXAMPLE 6 –
NIGHT GAMES

Set the context: darkness, nocturnal
    nature and sensory awareness
Sit-spot (short)
Lantern Stalk and variation
Predator
Return for a story by the fire

EXAMPLE 7 –
SEASHORE AT NIGHT

Sensory meditation
Buried Treasures
Cosmic Dance
Sit-spot
Fireside Sharing
Stories and sea shanties

EXAMPLE 8 –
STAR TREK ALL-NIGHT
ADVENTURE

Set the context: immersion
    in the night
Silent walk to a sunset viewpoint
Poem or reading
Sit-spot (30 minutes)
Sharing and reflection
Silent walk
Lay down on blankets
Silent beholding
Star narrative
Silent walk
Star navigational aids
Viewing Party (especially if the
    moon is rising/setting)
Silent walk
Pop-up Fireside (stories and
    poems about the night)
Napping/dreaming (1–2 hours)
Silent walk
Dawn Sit–spot
Final sharing and reflection

THE NIGHT PADDLE

Equipment required:
Canoes
Paddles
Buoyancy aids
Toilet bag
First aid kit
Torch with red filter
Red torchlight
Dry bags for valuables
Fire-making kit
Firewood (if required)
Pre-prepared meal for
  riverside dinner
Bananas
Chocolate bars or buttons
Trivet
Grill
Drinking water
Washing up bowls and materials
Tea-making facilities (if
  required)
Plates, cutlery, mugs (ask
  participants in advance to
  bring their own)
Ages: 6 and up (all participants
  must be able to swim)
Number of participants:
2–16

NOTE: you should only do this if you are an experienced canoer. Even if you are, navigating by night on the river brings new challenges and it's certainly something to practice on your own before you try to lead a group experience. I recommend getting advice from your local canoe club, and/or any canoe instructor. The likelihood is you will need accompanying by a professional, but they are easy to find, and hiring a professional instructor to accompany your group is not an expensive option.

For a truly exquisite experience of the night, you can't beat a night paddle. It is a sublime immersion into another perspective on all things nocturnal. I have guided more than a hundred of these magical journeys and the recipe of the river, its inhabitants, its fragrance, the stars and the silence conjures up an adventure that will both enchant and inspire.

Here, I describe how I lead a night paddle, but as with many of the activities in this book, it's an undertaking that allows for a certain amount of adaptability, to include a blend of other activities as part of the night paddling experience.

The boats I use, and which I recommend, are Canadian canoes, which can transport up to three adults, or a family of four if the children are under age eleven or so. Their advantage over kayaks is in their stability and the greater quantity of equipment they can carry. They are the ideal vessels to transport a group of up to twenty-four people, plus accompanying instructors.

(Take note, according to current British Canoe Union guidelines, the appropriate ratio for open flat water is one qualified instructor to four boats to ensure safety.)

The design concept of a night paddle includes an early evening trip up river for one to two hours, followed by a riverbank campfire supper, and then a silent paddle back under the cover of darkness. Here's an overview of how a night paddle unfolds, including some helpful tips for planning and leading the group.

Gather the group on the riverbank for a briefing on paddling the boats, the health and safety issues, and the plan for the evening. The best timing is to start out 60–90 minutes before dusk.

Once underway, after about 20–30 minutes paddling, gather the group together again for a check-in whilst in their boats (this is called 'rafting up'). Introduce them to the river, its wildlife and some expectations of what might be abroad at night in and around the river. Plan for this check-in and introductory remarks to last about 10 minutes, and then continue paddling upriver.

Arrange in advance for use of the spot where your group will stop to eat. It's best to find an open area on the riverbank where you have permission to light a campfire to heat up the pre-prepared meal. A delicious vegetarian stew is both easy to prepare, and easily portable in a large pot. Participants can sit on their buoyancy aids around the fire.

After the main meal, introduce some campfire cookery with the old classic of baked bananas. Lying the bananas on their side, slit open the skins with a knife and place two or three squares of chocolate inside (chocolate buttons are easy for this). To cook the bananas, place them (without foil) on a grill over the fire, or even straight in the embers where they will cook quite happily in their skins. When the chocolate has melted, they're ready, and a spoon is all that is required to scoop out the heavenly combination.

When everything is cleared away, tell a traditional tale around the fire (refer to the Campfire Time chapter on page 165 for story suggestions).

Give a briefing about the protocols of paddling back in the dark (your canoe instructor will probably want to make this presentation). Issue an invitation to avoid using any torches once everyone is on the water, in order to experience the night more fully. Once underway, issue another request for silence. This last invitation is well worth adhering to – it will convert a special experience into a sublime one. Be sure all members of the group understand that if anyone gets into difficulty, they can and should use their voices and torches as necessary.

Once arrived back at the starting point, load equipment back into vehicles/storehouse or whatever is required to complete the event.

Notes and Variants

Bad weather puts a damper on an event like this and so even though you can carry a lightweight tarp to throw up in the event of a shower, I recommend postponing rather than subjecting participants to adverse weather, which can also pose safety issues.

Similarly, you might want to choose a night where there is at least some moonlight to help night novices feel comfortable to paddle without resorting to their torches.

Bat detecting is often very fruitful on the river, with Daubenton's bats hunting low over the surface. It's a good idea to bring along a bat detector, or a more powerful torch to locate them in the dark.

You can also set up a one-way trip, rather than a round trip, depending on the length of the journey and the practical logistics pertaining to getting the boats/participants back to the starting point.

SEASHORE EXPERIENCE AND THE COSMIC DANCE

One of the most incredible places to be at dusk and into the night is the seashore. Over the years I have led many groups down to a sandy beach just as the 'changing of the guard' is taking place. Witnessing a sunset whilst

Equipment required:
An interesting-looking bag
  to carry everything
Throw line
First aid kit
3 ropes of different lengths,
  approximately 10 m
  (35 feet), 8 m (25 feet)
  and 6 m (20 feet)
Sketchbooks

Charcoal pencils
Pens
Crayons
Torches
Fire-making kit
Planispheres
Several Frisbees, painted gold
Ages: 8 and up
Number of participants:
12–25

the sea breeze caresses the skin, hearing the evensong of the wading birds giving their clarion calls to the sun, is a deep experience for any group as they sit in silence gazing over the ocean.

The seashore is also a potent threshold, full of prompts and promises, and like all transitional zones, is one of the most biodiverse natural places to be, with as much happening at night as during the day.

There are many ways to lead a seashore excursion. Here are suggestions of a format and activities that I've used successfully with groups.

Pack a bag in advance with the items on the equipment list above. (Take note, don't forget to check the local tide tables and risk-assess the beach for potential cut-off points.)

Start by asking the group to approach the beach in silence.

In the twilight, the first exploration of the beach is looking for 'buried treasure'. Hand out the gold Frisbees and invite the group to toss their six 'pieces of eight'. The idea is that wherever they land, you will always find little treasures.

For example, sea slaters are found as they emerge at dusk to feed on the seaweeds just above and below the high-water mark. Likewise, the masked crab is crepuscular in its habits, and sand-hoppers are ubiquitous, bouncing around like exploding popcorn in a hot pan. (For suggestions of seashore nature guides to learn more about the creatures that frequent beaches and shorelines, see the Links and Resources section on page 197.)

After a few rounds of throwing the gold, ask the group to gather together for the 'harvest'. Ask your companions to place some of their treasure on the upturned Frisbee 'trays' and then have a good old rummage through to see what has shown up.

Just as the daylight starts to fade and the moon rises, bring out the three ropes for the next activity: the Cosmic Dance.

Split up the group into three lots, with a different number of people in each one. Explain that each group will take the role of the sun, the Earth or the moon, and then they will act out the motion of these celestial bodies.

Give each group a rope (longest rope to the largest group, etc.) and ask them to form a circle by tying the ends of each rope together. The largest circle is the sun, which spins at the centre, the middle-sized group is the Earth, which spins on its axis and also orbits around the sun, and then the smallest, the moon, slowly rotates on its axis as it orbits around the Earth. There is lots of spinning and laughter as the groups simulate the spinning of these three celestial bodies.

Next, ask the groups to try it again and to demonstrate the effect of the moon upon the tides of the Earth. Here's how it works: each time the moon group passes a certain person in the Earth group, that Earth person should pull on the rope so it 'bulges' towards the moon, whilst the person opposite them on the Earth rope also pulls, making the rope bulge out as well. This represents centrifugal force in action. Explain that this occurs, of course, because the Earth is a 'blue planet', that contains so much water. All this bulging is the tidal movement of our oceans – in effect two constant waves moving round the planet.

Now attend to a bit more detail. When the moon and sun are in alignment there is an extra-large bulge, both when the moon is between the sun and Earth, and when it is on the opposite side of the Earth. These extra big bulges that occur at the spring tides result because the sun and moon's gravitational pull are working together, in alignment. When the moon, Earth and sun align at right angles, the bulge is minimal because they are working against each other; these are the neap tides.

When doing this on the beach, you can draw labels in the sand with a stick: an 'N' for neap, and an 'S' for spring. Needless to say, there is much fun to be had cavorting about in this way, but also a rather pleasing understanding of how the sun and moon are vital to the ocean tides.

For more detail and beautiful writing on the cosmic influences on our ocean, refer to sailor and surfer Jonathan White's book *Tides: The Science and Spirit of the Ocean*.

Following the Cosmic Dance activity, invite the group to a sit-spot to take in the darkening hour at the water's edge. Hand out sketchbooks and writing implements so they can write a poem or make a black-on-white sketch of the landscape of shadows, or perhaps the patterns of the celestial sky. Often the beach has little light pollution and so it's the perfect location to behold the landscape at night.

If you're lucky, you might look out to sea and see the bioluminescence make its ghostly appearance. These magical materialising millions are an otherworldly apparition, and will unfailingly induce awe and wonder. A single-celled algae, *Gonyaulax*, has remarkable bio-chemistry that produces this effervescence in the moment of reproduction.

One way to conclude the sit spot is with the haunting sound produced by blowing into a conch shell (practice in advance if you decide to do this). If you have arranged permission, build a bonfire on the beach and gather around it. Invite your companions to share personal reflections and perspectives to build a communal appreciation of the seashore environment.

To finish off the evening, hand out the planispheres. Small groups can work together to locate constellations. Or they may prefer to simply lie back and contemplate our tiny blue planet sailing through the vast ocean of space, whilst listening to the percussion of the waves breaking on the shore. These are truly magical moments.

Some good-old-fashioned storytelling can be a final bit of punctuation to the evening. Exploit the themes of the sea, voyages, stars, or the constellations. And of course, there will never be a better opportunity for some singing of sea shanties. Many of them having a call-and-response structure to get the singing up-and-running easily. See the Campfire Time chapter on page 165 for more possibilities.

DAWN CHORUS

Invite the group to experience the dawn by waking them up half an hour before first light, to hear the tender notes of the first birds. The important detail here, is to ensure that you are all seated in enough time to be ready to receive the very first song, as that is quite a moment to appreciate. Usually this will be just before we can detect the light changing, so best be in position 20 minutes beforehand.

Equipment required:
Sit mats
Ages: 9 and up
Number of participants:
Any

Even though you might get some pushback in making the invitation, I urge you to offer it anyway for those that are willing. Giving your first hour of attention to the changing of the guard is not to be underestimated, either as a solo experience, or shared with others. It's a heightened, rarefied time, and charged with feelings that garner connection and kinship.

Depending where you are, the first singer will vary, but more often than not, it will be the ubiquitous robin, or possibly a wren, dunnock, blackbird or song thrush, though I have heard skylarks too. The birds equipped with the largest eyes are the likely candidates, as they can take more advantage of the least amount of light.

What follows is a wonderful confluence of songs as each songbird throws its voice into the feral choir to greet the morning, its peak being about an hour after the earliest bird begins. Identifying the songsters is of course interesting, but it's really not essential if there is no ornithologist to distinguish which bird is which. It's enough to be simply present and paying attention with your ears.

DAWN DISPLAY

This follows the basics of the Sit-spot activity (see page 44), but an extra special ritual to conclude your dawn excursion is to arrange for the welcome discovery of an 'altar' of fruit on the trail back to your home or camp. It's beautifully arranged (by you and/or your helpers), with petals and foliage intertwined, as if the fairies themselves had designed it as a mysterious offering, and it arrives as a total surprise.

Once everyone is reassembled, make an invitation to sit in a circle around the fruity display, and partake of its 'sunlight energy', along with the warming rays of early morning. Some sharing is invited so each can reflect on their dawn experience, before heading back for breakfast.

Equipment required:
Sit mats
Ages: 9 and up
Number of participants:
Any

Now that's a way to start a day...

CHAPTER 7

Campfire Time

Among the Dagara, darkness is sacred. It is forbidden
to illuminate it, for light scares the Spirit away....
The one exception to this rule is the bonfire.

MALIDOMA PATRICE SOMÉ,
Of Water and the Spirit

There's nothing quite like sitting around the fire, but it's a rare experience for many people in our modern era. Long gone are the days when every evening the hearth would be the focus as the only source of light and heat. These days, electricity provides these comforts in almost every household, and thus we lose the shared experience of gathering around the fireside.

It's the proverbial icing on the cake to finish a nightwalk with some campfire time, and this chapter offers ways to enrich this experience further. It's beyond the scope of this book to cover all the possibilities, such as campfire cookery and firecraft, instead I concentrate on those bits and bobs that any group can undertake and enjoy during a campfire circle.

Setting the Tone

Setting the tone is important so that the group can presence the magic and mystery and moment of campfire time. After all, lest we take it for granted, fire is a pretty incredible phenomenon, and it hasn't always been at our disposal. I often begin a short narrative with the question, 'How long have human communities been sitting around a fire at night?' or, 'When do you think the first human fire was kindled?'

Wild guesses ensue, and when the answer comes it's a moment of perspective to consider how long our species have depended on fire. The role of fire throughout human history is explored with another question: 'What possibilities did the first fire bring for humanity?' This invitation solicits plenty of willing hands offering the obvious answers of 'light', 'warmth' and 'cooking'. More thought brings up other everyday uses such as electricity and locomotion, and then the different crafts and technologies that fire enabled such as pottery, glass and metalworking. It's a fun exercise to challenge the group to see whether they can get to twenty different uses. Some that are often missed include land management, hunting, tanning, hygiene, and food preservation and flavouring. In fact, this exercise ends up creating a very extraordinary picture of just how dependent humans have become on this primal element, even today. Even our rituals and celebrations make use of flame and fireworks. There is almost nothing we do, or have, that can't be traced back to some aspect of a fire burning somewhere off stage. And, in case you are interested, archaeological evidence from China so far suggests that humans have been purposefully generating fire for at least 700,000 years.

In terms of the Earth's story, there's been 'fire in the belly' of the planet since the beginning, and fire has played its part on the Earth's surface for much longer than humans have been around.

As an outdoorsman and a storyteller, I have long been fascinated with the relationship between fire and stories, and although I might be making an imaginative leap here, I reckon that one development directly influenced another. In other words, with the prospect of safely sitting around a fire, protected from animals higher up the food chain, humans earned themselves leisure time in the evenings, and it would be natural to assume that communication developments followed. It's only a short step from here to imagine them telling each other the 'story of the day'. These early narratives would have been prone to the same wild exaggerations and caricature that we give anecdotal stories today. I can easily imagine a gradual progression into the broad art of storytelling. Well, that's my version of things anyway and nobody has yet proved me wrong, so I'm sticking to it.

Fireside Traditions

It seems to me that all human cultures from all corners of the globe would have sat around the campfire and developed their fireside traditions through sharing story and song. In our own recent tradition, the fireside is also the place to enjoy word games and recitations, and so here are some of my own favourite things to do around the campfire.

Storytelling

The spoken word obtains a particular clarity at night, without the competing distractions and diversions of the daylight. The story transports listeners away from the toil of the day's labour into fanciful realms of wonder. A deeper listening is possible in the dark and also our imaginative capacity is heightened – what we cannot see, we invent. We've been telling stories at night since 'before the first before', as the storytellers say...

One of the earliest literary examples of our collective fear of and fascination with the dark is the terrific old Anglo-Saxon narrative of *Beowulf*, with its conceit of a monster emerging out of the dark to wreak a terrible havoc upon the people.

Thrilling stuff, and the tale still resonates because it is universal – who hasn't at some point in their life, and especially as a child, cowered under the sheets as we imagined the terrifying things that lurked in the darkness poised to pounce upon us and tear us to pieces? I certainly have. Homer's *Iliad* tells us that even the mighty Zeus trembled before the prospect of Nyx, the goddess of the 'all-subduing' night.

And yet, despite the terror, we invite frightening stories into our lives, these days in the form of the hugely popular genre of horror movies. But let me tell you that around the evening campfire, the same phenomena manifest in the endless requests for a good old ghost story. It's as if we *want* to be scared. And, after I've told one ghost story, without fail, the youngsters ask if I have something more scary. 'What's the scariest story you know?' they sometimes say. 'Tell us that one!'

As a professional storyteller I exercise some prudence and discernment in the choice of material for a crowd of youngsters, lest the bravado that is bolstered by the warmth and company around the fireside deserts the individual sleeping alone in the tent at night. I don't want to invite the 'night terrors'. Stories that stir up the idea of ghosts and ghouls but are light in tone easily hit the spot. That's not to say I won't pull a dark and unsettling tale out of the treasure bag of stories for an adult audience!

There's a lot to say about how to tell stories, far more than I can explain here. I'll content myself with offering some basic advice to get you going, and trust you to find your way. In a way, it's a very simple craft and doesn't need complicating. But in other ways, there's a lot more to it than you might think.

Telling a story to kids is a good way to start. The fireside is the perfect setting, for various reasons. The dim lighting feels very supportive and the fire itself invites another focus, so that you as the storyteller don't squirm 'in the spotlight'. A classic 'beginner's mistake' is to embark on telling a

Storytelling Tips

- Listen to a variety of storytellers to pick up styles and techniques.
- If you find a story you like in a book, remember that storytelling is an oral tradition, and spoken stories are different from written ones. Don't try to memorise the story as written. Instead, tell it in your own words.
- Only tell stories you like.
- Practise out loud – find a listener, or take the story for a walk and tell the trees.
- Use eye contact – try to make eye contact with everyone in the group as you tell the story.
- 'Report' what you 'see'; that means, see the story unfold in your mind's eye and tell the audience what you see.
- Use rhythm, repetition and rhyme where appropriate. Alliteration also helps serve the storytelling.
- Allow yourself not to be an expert straightaway – like any worthwhile skill, it takes time.

long story. Take my advice: don't try to tell anything longer than a five-minute tale until you are more practised.

When all is said and done, the way to tell stories is to simply launch in – and if you are faithful to the tale, it will serve you well, and your audience. In other words, let the story do its own work – think of yourself like a reporter, explaining an event that really happened. This helps to reduce any performance anxiety. In fact, don't perform (unless you have this quality in you already), *tell* the story. Then, pay attention to how the story is landing with your listeners, so that you can constantly make adjustments each time you tell it. By the twentieth time you've told it, it will settle into a pattern and you can begin to play around with variations to keep it fresh each time.

Storytelling Games

Whether you tell a solo story or not, a fun way to meet the need for some campfire storytelling is to invite the group to collaborate to improvise one. There are several ways to pursue this.

One way to begin is by offering up the first line yourself. Then, the person sitting next to you adds another line, or several. You can decide the guidelines: whether to limit each person to a single line or to leave everyone free to develop the storyline further than that if they wish. There are pros and cons to each approach. To take the pressure off the introverts in the group, there can be an option to 'pass'. The story should be complete when it comes back around to whoever started it off.

> *When television came in through the front door, the stories went out the back door.* **ISLE OF LEWIS** saying

Another group story follows the same form, but the story develops one word at a time. This will probably need to travel a few times around the circle to complete, depending on the number of players. Another variation on these forms is for each player to offer their contribution and then point to someone to go next. This of course prevents any prior planning and relies even more on improvisational skills.

Here are some tips to help make group storytelling effective and enjoyable. With groups of children, particularly 6–12 year olds, there's a tendency for the boys to steer the story towards death or violence. This can have the effect of ending the story prematurely, and therefore unsatisfactorily, and being rather predictable. You may want to introduce a few rules. For example, the story cannot include any mention of weapons or killing. You may even decide that there should be no recourse to magical skills or deeds, as this can also become surprisingly unsatisfactory if it is overplayed. I encourage you to experiment with this art form to see what emerges. One thing is for sure, whatever rules you set for a storytelling game, the kids love playing them!

Stories to Tell

The nature of the oral tradition is such that that stories accompanied travellers, merchants and migrants wherever they went, and were shared and swapped around the fireside. It's an old saying that when a storyteller tells a story it becomes theirs, but when it's been told it's given away as a gift to the community that hears it. That said, I offer every story I tell with an understanding and respect for the cultures that brought them. It's my belief that this helps to celebrate and differentiate between traditions.

May this be so.

THE DISAPPEARANCE OF THE MOON

This is an example of the nomadic aspect of stories, which end up being claimed by people living in different regions, sometimes thousands of miles apart. It's also a testimony to the pure orality of the tales as they morph and change as they travel. This is a Devon version, which I have located on Dartmoor.

When the moon looked down upon old Dartmoor, she never saw the 'other folk', the pixies that lurked in the shadows and caused such mischief, so she decided to come down to see for herself if the stories she'd heard were true.

She disguised herself in that great dark cloak of hers and she came down through the night to land upon the tussocks, high upon the moorland. She walked from tussock to stone peering into the inky blackness and she saw them alright, those strange little pixies, with their funny hats and pointed boots. 'So,' she said, 'the stories are true!' And as she said that, she slipped over, and as she fell, she grabbed a branch from a tiny hawthorn tree growing up out of the peat, to steady herself. But when she tried to get up, the branch had twisted around her wrist, and she was tied and tangled and she was snared. As she writhed and wriggled, the shadows moved towards her, and she batted them away, but there were so many. During this struggle suddenly she heard a man cry out over the moor, 'Help! For Pity's sake, help me!' The moon couldn't see where he was, so she threw back her head so the hood of her cloak fell back casting light from her face. The pixies scuttled off to the shadows and she saw in the distance a man was waist deep in one of the deep Dartmoor bogs, he was being dragged down by pixies who then vanished away from the light. The man was able to haul himself up and away into the night. The moon struggled on but, try as she might, she could not free herself, and soon she fell exhausted onto her knees, and her head sank onto her chest and the hood fell over her face. Then, in the darkness the pixies came and dragged her down into one of those dark pools, and the moon was gone.

Over the next days and nights, the people wondered where the moon had gone, and were troubled by the visitations of all of the strange and wicked things that were emboldened by the deep dark. The pixies were coming into the villages and causing mischief, and some took to leaving their homes and gathering in the tavern. One night, all the talk was about the vanished moon, when suddenly a stranger who was listening in the corner cried out, 'Of course! Why didn't I think about it before?' All attention went to him while he told his story. 'I was making my way across the moor on one of those blackest of nights, and I lost my way and fell into one of them dreadful bogs. The pixies came for me and I thought my last day on Earth had come. I shouted for help, and suddenly, out of nowhere there shone a light. Bright it was, like the light of a full moon. Well, I was able to escape and find the path and run for home. Now that I think about it, I'm wondering if that light could have been the moon herself?'

The next day a delegation of people agreed to visit Old Meg of the Moor. Some said she was wise, others said she was a witch, and a few thought she was plain crazy. She lived high up on the blanket bogs in a little reed-thatched cottage all on its own. When they entered she was hunched over the fire, stirring the cauldron with one of her eyes looking down into the pot, and the other gazing up through the smoke hole. The people told her about the vanished moon. Old Meg was silent for a long time. Suddenly she shouted, 'This is what you must do! Tonight you must cut hazel sticks and put those in your left hands. You must light lanterns and put those in your right hand. You must place round stones under your tongues and head up on to the highest hills. There you must look for a cross. Then a coffin. Then there will be a light!'

'As strange as they are, we will do those things,' said the villagers, and they left. That night a brave deputation of men, cut sticks, lit lanterns, placed stones under their tongues, and headed out into the deep dusk, up the hill, into the deeper dark. They huddled like partridges, swinging their lanterns before them as the shadows chased around the fringes of the lamplight. Further and further they went, hearing the distant village church bell grow fainter. Finally, around midnight, one of the men shouted and pointed. They saw the little hawthorn tree that had grown shaped like a cross. Beyond that, they saw a huge, long, black stone looking for all the world that night, like a coffin, and on top of the stone there were a swarm of pixies. The men crossed themselves, and said the Lord's prayer, for the sake of the cross. Then they said it backwards for the sake of the pixies. Then, they moved over to the stone, as the pixies scurried away from the lantern light. They rolled the heavy stone over, and saw a bright light beneath. For a moment, they gazed down upon the face of the moon; she was the most beautiful thing they had ever seen. But the light was too bright and as the stone rolled away, they covered their eyes. When they took their hands away from their faces, they nodded and grinned in the light of a full moon, now riding the sky.

Ever since then, the people say that in her gratitude, the moon shines brightest on Dartmoor. Mind you, on the moonless nights, you still have to be careful about those mischievous pixies!

NIGHT AND DAY

This is my version of a traditional tale told by the Nez Perce people of indigenous America. My thanks to their ancient tradition and to all the countless tales shared around the fireside by storytellers from all traditions around the world.

In the oldest of times, when people and animals were one, there was no night and no day. The animal people were endlessly quarrelling about which was which, and how long it should last.

Bear and wolf were there, frog and toad, too. Eagle and wren, badger and fox, mouse and vole. There were many voices that argued for and against the length of the day and the length of the night.

Bear believed there should be five days of light and only one of darkness, and that dawn should come only on the fifth day. But Badger was not in favour of this. 'Brother,' he said, 'it is better to forage and find under the cover of darkness, let us therefore have ten days of darkness and only one of light.' Owl was in agreement, but went a step further. 'Why not have night for one year with one day at the end?' This was not popular with the blackbirds and thrushes, and the weasels and stoats preferred more daylight than darkness.

Well, they argued and argued, and no resolution seemed close. Finally, frog spoke up for fairness and equality and said, 'I propose they should be divided evenly, and that we should compromise with one day followed by one night.' This was greeted by howls and squeaks and barks and growls of derision, as the animals favouring the night pressed their case. It went back and forth between the day-loving animals and the night-loving animals until it was decided that one representative from each side should battle it out, with the one who could keep arguing the longest, declared the winner.

Frog and owl faced each other, and began to present their arguments. They argued, harangued and cajoled each other, urging the other to see sense and agree. Frog was the more patient and, after a long time of debating the issue, owl lost his appetite for the fight.

Frog was declared the winner, and then decreed that, 'From now on, there will be one day followed by one night.'

Since that time, this has been the way of things. Frog still sings of victory, especially at night, just to annoy the owl. The owl, hoots in dismay at losing the argument.

BAT HIDES FROM THE SUN

Because stories live in a nebulous orality, and because they have migrated with countless travellers and tribes who have shared them around countless campfires over thousands of years, it is not always possible to identify the specific source of a story. This one though, comes to me via Alida Gersie, and originally from the continent of Africa.

In the time before time, before the first before, bat lived with his mother, who one day became ill, and in the following days became even more sick. Bat called deer to attend to his ailing mother, but deer took one look at her and said, 'She needs the medicine of the sun. Only the sun can help your mother.'

The next day, bat journeyed to visit the sun at his house, but it was late morning when he met the sun, already on the road. 'Please help, my mother is sick and needs some medicine,' said bat, but the sun said, 'It is too late, I have already left my house. Come tomorrow.'

So bat returned home, and slept the night. In the morning, earlier than before, he met the sun again already on the road. 'Once I have left my house, I cannot return,' said the sun. 'That is where I keep the medicine. Come again in the morning.'

Again bat returned home, and again he left even earlier the next morning. But again he was too late. The sun had already left his house. Each day he tried, each day leaving earlier, and each day he was sent back. His mother grew gravely ill, and by the seventh day, she had died.

Bat was grief-stricken, and angry with the sun. 'If he had made some medicine for her, she would not have died! The sun is responsible for the death of my mother!'

Many of the beasts came to share in bat's mourning, and when it was time to bury her, they asked to look upon her face, as they always did before a body went into the grave.

But, when they saw her, they said, 'No, we cannot bury her. She isn't one of us. Look! She has a face like us, but she has wings like a bird. You must call the birds to bury her.' And they left.

Bat called to the birds, and when they looked upon bat's mother they saw her teeth and they said, 'Yes, she is like us because she has wings, but look at those teeth! No bird has teeth – she has no beak. We cannot bury her,' and they left bat alone. The ants came and entered his mother's body. Bat spoke to himself:

'I blame the sun. The sun should have made medicine for my mother. The sun has killed her. Now the sun is my enemy, and I will never look upon the sun's face again, nor will I greet him ever again. I shall hide from the sun. I will hide in the darkness. I will visit nobody.'

And that is why bats only emerge as the sun is setting, lest they are forced to greet the sun's smiling face.

Campfire Songs

Campfire songs are the bees' knees for groups that include children. These are songs in which everyone sings along rather than songs sung as solos. Not that there's anything wrong with solo singing, but campfire time is about building community, and so songs that are easy to learn are the name of the game. It's a little dispiriting for the group when it takes a long time to teach a song, and it can dampen the mood. Better to select those that are instantly graspable with simple tunes and words. There are some that are call-and-response, which are perfect for this, but plenty more to choose from.

It's worth learning how to teach a song well – how to be succinct but effective. The gist of song leading is to slow down and bring everyone along at the same pace. Sing a line, then have everyone sing it back to you. Then repeat. Then sing the next line. Then repeat. Then try the two lines together. Repeat. And so on and so forth, building the capacity to memorise the lines. Listen to the group's progress, and adapt your pace accordingly. If you are teaching a round, have the group sing it through a few times in unison before attempting to break them up into parts.

There would be little point in writing out song lyrics here, because what is a song without its melody? Instead, I refer you to the Links and Resources section on page 197 for some guidance. There's an amazing number of websites where you can sift through a wide repertoire of songs and choose those that are appropriate to your level of experience and/or age of the group you want to sing with. One of the longest-running camps for children is the Forest School Camps, which began its wonderful initiative way back in the 1940s. A link to their treasure trove of campfire songs can be found at www.virtualcampfire.co.uk.

One song that is a sheer delight to offer into a stargazing experience, if you are that way inclined, is the classic 'Galaxy Song' written for *Monty Python* by Eric Idle and John Du Prez. It contains a considerable amount of astronomical information and will help everyone connect to the wonder of the universe. (Note there is now an updated version, as the original was written in 1983.) You may end up singing it as a solo, but encourage anyone who knows it to join in.

Nighwatchman's Songs

The lyrics below are three traditional nightwatchman's songs that have trickled down the strata of years. There are no recordings of these songs, and although they clearly belong in a bygone era, are particularly congruent for our practice of watching the night. In the old days, there was always a nightwatchman appointed to towns and villages whose job it was to make the night rounds with his lantern, seeking out and warding off trouble and threats to the sleeping population.

You will have to make up your own melodies for these songs, or you can simply recite them aloud as you would a poem.

SING AND REJOICE THE DAY IS GONE

Sing and rejoice the day is gone,
And the wholesome night appears
In which the constable on the throne
Of trusty bench doth with his peers
The comely watchmen sound of health
Sleep for the good of commonwealth.

HO WATCHMEN, HO

Ho watchmen, ho
Twelve is the clock,
God keep our town,
from fire and brand,
and hostile hand,
Twelve is the clock.

A LIGHT HERE MAIDS, HANG OUT YOUR LIGHT

A light here maids, hang out your light,
And see your horns be clear and bright
That so your candle clear may shine
Continuing from six to nine
That honest men may walk along
And see to pass safe without wrong.

Auntie Jane

As you lead this song, explain to the group that it a call and response song: you sing a phrase, and then the group sings it back to you. The group should also imitate the actions as you introduce them. The actions are cumulative, by the end everyone should be wobbling everything they've got – everywhere!

When Auntie came back from old Hong Kong
She brought me back a game of ping pong
(Mime 'ping pong' with your right hand)
When Auntie came back from Old Japan
she brought me back a lovely fan
('Fan' with left hand)
When Auntie came back from Old Venice
She brought me back a game of tennis
(Mime moving your head left and right watching a ball)
When Auntie came back from Aberdeen
She brought me back a sewing machine
(Mime moving one leg up n down the treadle)
When Auntie came back from Aberdare
She brought me back a rocking chair
(Rock forwards and backwards)
When Auntie came back from Timbuctoo
She brought me back a TWIT LIKE YOU!
(Point to everyone in the group)

Campfire Games

As with campfire songs, there's a host of games to glean from online resources, but here are a few of my favourites to enrich the time spent around the campfire. Some of them are pattern recognition games – confounding games in which one person begins a verbal or physical sequence and the object of the game is to guess what the hidden cue is in order to be able to successfully join in. Generally they can be played with ages eight and up, but that's not to say younger children could not join in. Supporting adults can help them figure out the pattern by caricaturing their responses. That said, adults can be the last to pick it up and of course their frustration about 'not getting it' only adds to the overall enjoyment!

There are endless variations and you can easily make up your own. You could add a verbal cue, such as always saying 'um' before you speak, or a visual clue, like having to have your legs crossed to be 'in the club'.

This is a What?

Start with two items in your hands, such as a stick and a stone.

The object of the game is to pass the items in opposite directions around the circle. That seems simple enough, but because of the form of the game, it usually ends up with great confusion and hilarity (which is what makes it so fun)!

Begin with a demonstration to establish the form of the game.

Turn to one of the people sitting next to you. Hand them the stick (or whatever it is) and say, 'This is a stick.'

They reply, 'A what?'

You repeat, 'A stick'

They reply, 'Oh, it's a stick!' They then take the stick and turn to the person next to them, and say, 'This is a stick.' And when the reply comes, 'a what', they have to turn back to you and ask, 'A what?' and when you repeat, 'It's a stick!' they pass this on with, 'It's a stick!'

This pattern is then repeated, so that 'a what' keeps travelling back to you, to say 'a stick!' which then travels back to the next person.

You then demonstrate the same thing, with the person sitting on your other side, handing them the stone. 'This is a stone,' 'A what?' 'A stone.' 'Oh! It's a stone!' And so on.

After the demonstration, the game begins for real. Take possession of the stick and stone again. Begin by turning to the person on your left to send the stick clockwise, and as soon as that is underway, immediately start the process with the person on your right to send the stone anticlockwise. The timing of this start is tight, and you must concentrate to get it up and running, but it does work and is part of the entertainment.

Once the pattern is established, much pleasure is derived from the repetition and the inevitable chaos and confusion that ensues, especially when both objects arrive together at the mid-point of the circle. The people unfortunately positioned there will trip over their tongues as they figure out the logic and pattern. And, like many games, it does not have to be got right – it's just for fun!

One Spot

This utterly hilarious game is sure to break the ice in any group setting. It's one of those games that starts slowly and surely, but as mistakes are made, begins to unravel into an unruly, enjoyable chaos.

Using a cork marked with charcoal (or a non-toxic paint), the leader starts by putting a spot on the forehead of each player. Sitting in a circle, the leader as 'player one' introduces themselves as 'one-spot', the player alongside then introduces herself as 'two-spot', the next player is 'three-spot', and so on around the circle. This appellation does not change during the game. What does change, however, is the number of spots marked on their face as the game progresses.

The game starts with the invigilator saying, 'one-spot with one spot to number seven-spot with one spot'. Number seven-spot would then have to respond by passing on to another, for example, 'Number seven-spot with one-spot to number twelve with one-spot.' The game ensues, until someone fluffs their lines in some way. Every time someone makes a mistake, hesitates, gets the words wrong or laughs, etc., they are given another mark on their face by the leader. Therefore, the person sitting in place number seven, if they had been deemed to have made a mistake, would now say, 'Seven-spot with two spots,' every time they are involved. The thing is, everyone's numbers keep changing as more mistakes are made, and more charcoal spots are added. It becomes increasingly difficult for everyone to keep track of who has what number of spots and the process degenerates into much laughter and confusion.

Hot Sticks

There's not much more fun and fascination to be had than thrusting a long, thin stick in the fire and then, in your own safe space in the dark, waving it around to 'draw' in the night sky. I know, I know – it's not very 'Health & Safety' is it? But kids enjoy it so much, and whilst it is not appropriate in fire-risk areas (of which Britain generally isn't), I hope you will forgive me for recommending it as a cheeky little activity.

'Through the Green Glass Door'

In this game, the only words to get you 'in the club', are words that contain double letters, for example, bottle, happy and brolly. Each player has a go at what they can and can't 'see', using the same phrase and are immediately told if they are in the club or not. As the game progresses more and more players figure out the 'code' and the pattern slowly dawns on more of the players until everyone has sussed it, or if not, until the leader ends it.

For example, it could start with: 'Through the green glass door, I can see the breeze, but I can't see the wind...'

Correct responses might be: 'Through the green glass door, I can see little things, but I can't see big things.' Or, 'Through the green glass door, I can see grass but I can't see flowers.'

The Magic Pen

Here's a great game for youngsters that includes a visual prompt. Begin by describing the concept of the magic pen (which of course is imaginary). The magic pen can draw anything, and while you hold it you can be an amazing artist, but only if you use it 'properly' – which is the object of this game, for the group to figure out how it's used 'properly'.

The riddler declares what s/he will draw and then air-sculpts a drawing for everyone to see, and, even though it's a pantomime, does it with great care. S/he then hands the pen with a show of ceremony to the next person, who attempts to figure out what is a 'proper' use of the pen. Of course, despite the care taken to copy exactly the process, it fails to impress the riddler and the pen passes from one to the next, each trying something different to make the pen 'work'.

Sometimes, the riddler will be asked to demonstrate again, and the puzzlement and entertainment continues until the 'code' is cracked.

The protocol then of course is to enjoy being 'in the club' without making it too obvious what the hidden cue is.

The cue in this case, is to always say 'thank you' when receiving the pen. Some will say this automatically but their ensuing 'success' with the magic pen is unwitting, and they may not be able to repeat their success when asked, adding to the general confusion and entertainment of all.

Riddles

Riddles are another playful interaction through which you can explore the theme of darkness, and everyone enjoys a good riddle. You can begin with a mysterious but truly astronomical riddle, which is the perfect puzzler before a nightwalk. If nobody guesses it, then better to keep them guessing until the end – or, better still, send them home with some interesting homework to do.

That first riddle, of course, is the ultimate teaser…

Why is it dark?

(The profound and unexpected answer to this can be found in the Epilogue at the end of the book.)

There's a protocol with riddles, which is not to give away the answer – well, at least not without some sort of forfeit. Be sure to ask that if anyone already knows the answer, they 'keep schtum' to preserve the fun. If the kids are just too desperate to know the answer, you can offer a forfeit as a penalty – playfully suggest they 'buy' the answer from you by doing the washing up or emptying the camp toilet in the morning!

Classic Riddles

Here are five of my favourite campfire riddles. No need to stick with these, though – find your own favourites, too!

> You feed me, and I live.
> You give me something to drink, and I die.
> What am I?
> (**A fire**)

> In daytime I lie pooled about,
> At night I cloak like a mist.
> I creep inside shut boxes and
> Inside your tightened fist.
> You see me best when you can't see,
> For I do not exist.
> What am I?
> (**Darkness**)

There's someone that I'm always near,
Yet in the dark I disappear.
To this one only I am loyal,
Though in his wake I'm doomed to toil.
He feels me not (we always touch);
If I were lost, he'd not lose much.
And now I come to my surprise,
For you are he – but who am I?
(**Your shadow**)

I was born millions of years ago,
And yet, I am never more than a month old
What am I?
(**The moon**)

At night they come without being fetched
And by day they are lost without being stolen.
(**Stars**)

Lateral Thinkers

Not quite a traditional riddle, but along the same lines and a wonderful conundrum for a group to solve are the 'lateral thinkers', where you are asked to make sense of something that does not seem at first to make sense. In these forms, to help you, and to make it more interactive, you can ask the riddler questions, but only ones that can be answered with a yes or no.

TWO PADDLERS

Two people in a canoe, paddling through a desert.
One at the front turns to the other and says,
'Wears (where's) your paddle?'
The other replies, 'It sure does!'

How does this make sense?

Answer: In this one, it's the play on the words wears/where's that is key. To solve it, the group must explain the response, because everyone assumes that there is a question – 'Where's your paddle?' – whereas in fact, it's a statement: 'Wears your paddle.' The rationale being that paddling through sand would indeed wear down your paddle...

HOW MANY WOMEN?

Two mothers and two daughters stopped on a bridge to look at their reflections in the river below.

Only three figures looked back from the water...

How could this be, and why?

Answer: There were three women: a grandmother, a mother and her daughter.

DOOR KEEPERS

There are two doors, and in front of each door, there are two brothers who are the doorkeepers. One door leads to heaven, and one leads to hell, but you don't know which is which. You are allowed one question to one of the doorkeepers to find out which is the right door to go through: the door to heaven.

To help you find the right question to ask, all there is to know about the doorkeepers is that one of them always tells the truth, and the other one always lies.

What question are you going to ask?

Answer: the question to ask either one of the brothers is, 'Which door would your brother tell me to go through?' You then go through the opposite door to the one suggested.

Poems

For the right group profile, a little 'garnish' for a nightwalk is supplied by a poem to set a particular tone, or simply to provide a final punctuation on the evening. It's more for adult ears, of course, but older children will tolerate short poems. An effective recitation can serve to heighten the mystery and/ or anticipation, even if the deeper meaning or resonance is lost on them.

Here are two of my favourites that will work on different levels, depending on the profile and culture of the group you are escorting. I also include a longer list of poems that have themes of darkness and night. Find your own, too!

BLESSED BE THE NIGHT

Twilight is a time for sharing – and a time for
remembering – sharing the fragrance of the
cooling earth – the shadows of the gathering
dusk –

Here our two worlds meet and pass – the
frantic sounds of man grow dimmer as the light
recedes – the unhurried rhythm of the other
world swells in volume as the darkness
deepens –

It is not strange that discord has
no place in this great symphony of sound –
it is not strange that a sense
of peace descends upon all living things –
it is not strange that
memories burn more brightly – as the things of
substance lose their line and form in the softness
of the dark –

Twilight is a time for sharing – and a
time for remembering – remembering the things of
beauty wasted by our careless hands – our frequent

disregard of other living things – the many songs
unheard because we would not listen –

Listen tonight with all the
wisdom of your spirit – listen too with
all the compassion of your heart –
lest there come another night –
where there is only silence –

A great
and
total
silence –

WINSTON O. ABBOTT

SWEET DARKNESS
When your eyes are tired
the world is tired also.

When your vision has gone,
no part of the world can find you.

Time to go into the dark
where the night has eyes
to recognize its own.

There you can be sure
you are not beyond love.

The dark will be your home
tonight.

The night will give you a horizon
further than you can see.

You must learn one thing.
The world was made to be free in.

Give up all the other worlds
except the one to which you belong.

Sometimes it takes darkness and the sweet
confinement of your aloneness
to learn

anything or anyone
that does not bring you alive

is too small for you.

DAVID WHYTE, *The House of Belonging*

There are so many more wonderful poems about the night. Here's a list of some of my favourites:

'The Night Traveler' by Mary Oliver
'Winter's Cloak' by Joyce Rupp
'The Dark Hours of My Being' by Rainer Maria Rilke
'The Night' by Rainer Maria Rilke
'Let This Darkness Be a Bell Tower' by Rainer Maria Rilke
'The Birthnight' by Walter de la Mare
'Let Evening Come' by Jane Kenyon
'Mother Night' by James Weldon Johnson
'Summer Stars' by Carl Sandburg
'To Night' by Percy Bysshe Shelley
'But Men Loved Darkness Rather Than Light' by Richard Crashaw
'A Summer Night' by Elizabeth Drew Stoddard
'In the Dark of Night' by Raymond A. Foss
'Hymn to the Night' by Henry Wadsworth Longfellow
'Flowers of Darkness' by Frank Marshall Davis
'Dark Night' by Frank Bidart

'Coffin Path Poem' by Helen Farish
'When the Dark Comes Down' by Lucy Maud Montgomery
'In a Kind Darkness' by Jon Fosse
'We Grow Accustomed to the Dark' by Emily Dickinson
'To the Evening Star' by William Blake
'The Moon' by Robert Louis Stevenson
'Elegy' by D. H. Lawrence
'To Sleep' by John Keats
'A Night in the Field' by Jay Parini
'Stars' by Emily Bronte
'Moon-Lover' by Robert William Service
'The Moon Rises' by Federico García Lorca
'The Harvest Moon' by Ted Hughes
'Sonnet LXXXI (And Now You're Mine)' by Pablo Neruda
'Moonrise' by Gerard Manley Hopkins
'The Starlight Night' by Gerard Manley Hopkins
'The Owner of the Night' by Mark Doty
'Night Sky' by Don Bogen
'Night Blooming Jasmine' by Giovanni Pascoli
'Stars' by Christian Barter
'The Nightingale' by Samuel Taylor Coleridge
'There was a Boy' by William Wordsworth
'The Sun Has Long Been Set' by William Wordsworth
'Nocturne' by Gwendolyn Bennett
'The Night Is Still' by Edith Matilda Thomas
'Blood Moon' by Elizabeth Jacobson
'Wonder' by Mei-mei Berssenbrugge
'The Darkness' by Aiden Young

Dawn

A night-time of activities starts at twilight and, by the time the campfire dies down, we find ourselves finishing at dawn.

Daybreak, sunup, cockcrow, crack of day. Whether you've been out all night, or have got up early to catch the end of the night, the turning of the tide at dawn is no less breathtaking than the exhale of the day at dusk. The moment where you can detect the first subtle shift of light is usually the stillest, quietest part of the night, as if everything is holding its breath just before it all changes, and all the consequence of the day flows in. This is also the delicious moment of the first song, as the bird kingdom greets the inrushing tide of light with arias of their own making.

You'll see the stars slowly extinguish, the inky black sky turn imperceptibly to indigo and then a rainbow of colours. A view of the east is an advantage, as is a clearish sky, but it's not a prerequisite. Just sit and wait. Listen with your ancient ears and watch with your animal eyes, the slow retreat of the dark, and the processional revelation of the dawn. It's quite a tango.

Birdsong is one of the great joys of the outdoors at dawn. If you could follow that wave of dawn birdsong eastward by physically travelling at the pace with which the dawn is rising, you would travel with the soundtrack of a dawn chorus constantly in your ears. Imagine then, that our planet is permanently caressed by this sound wave of birdsong as each habitat greets the dawn progressively. Although there are patches of the Earth that have few or no birds, it's a sweet thought that this endless serenading has been a constant wave of song for hundreds of thousands of years. Evolution guiding the journey from planet Earth to planet Song…

So let's now sit together, in reverence of these songs of praise and attentive and thankful to the receding tide of darkness, to welcome all the possibilities of yet another new dawn. Leaving the last words to Walt Whitman:

> *Preceded by an immense star, almost unearthly in its effusion of white splendor, with two or three long unequal spoke-rays of diamond radiance, shedding down through the fresh morning air below – an hour of this, and then the sunrise.*

Why is it Dark?

O ur contemporary scientific 'creation myth' informs us that it all began with a Big Bang. Curiously, this is analogous to the Christian story of the Beginning: '"Let there be light!" And there was light.'

A two thousand-year-old Mediterranean myth invites us to believe that the world came into being with 'seven laughs', the first one being the light. Contemporary science would have us believe that it took less than a billionth of a second for this 'first laugh' to occur – for an infinitesimally small, hot seed of energy to flare forth and become all the matter that exists in the universe today.

You know, I'm not sure which explanation is more believable…

But what about the end of creation? What is that story? Our geniuses from the world of astrophysics are keen to speculate, and some of them hypothesise that it will culminate rather neatly, like all good stories, in a return to the 'beginning'.

By working out mathematical equations of the structures and patterns of movement in celestial bodies, astrophysicists have arrived at a rather dramatic conclusion: Our life-sustaining star, the sun, will burn itself out and the Earth will float in a frozen, sterile orbit around an extinguished star. But before that apocalypse there will be an even more dramatic one, because our wild and wondrous universe is expanding in all directions at an accelerating rate, which looks set to continue. This means that all the stars and planets are moving away from each other, and thus I like to think that there will come a time when if there were any inhabitants left on the Earth (this isn't likely to happen, of course) would look up into a vast and empty dark night sky, with no twinkling points of light to be seen.

And this phenomenon of expansion explains why there is darkness. It was a clarification of astronomical theory that became known as Olbers' paradox.

Let's back up to set the stage for Olbers' paradox. In 1610, German astronomer Johannes Kepler received a copy of Galileo's little book, *Sidereus Nuncius* (Starry Messenger) in which Galileo argued that the universe must be infinite and therefore contained an infinite number of stars. Kepler took issue with this idea because, in his estimation, if there truly were an infinite number of stars, the night-time would be ablaze with the light from those countless celestial bodies. In 1826, another German astronomer, Heinrich Olbers, reasserted this argument, essentially stating that if the universe is infinite and uniformly sprinkled with stars, *then there should be no night*.

The ultimate resolution of this paradox did not arrive until the advent of twentieth-century scientific instrumentation. Despite desperate attempts by scientists to test and undermine the logic in Olbers' paradox, it was finally agreed that he was correct, and the universe must indeed, by the firm laws of physics, be bound in time and space.

Flippin' 'eck!

So, if I understand the physicists correctly, if the galaxies were not galloping away from each other, more and more starlight would have arrived into our night sky, making the night blaze much, much brighter. But because everything is stretching away from us, it maintains and slowly extends the vast distances in between, keeping us in the dark, and able to behold the starry sky at night.

So that's the answer to the riddle posed at the beginning of the book: the reason it is dark at night is because the universe is expanding. And because of that expansion, we can imagine a far distant future that has Earth floating very much 'alone' in space.

Two theories regarding the eventual climax of our expanding universe compete for science's attention. One states that the universe will continue to expand, stretching out so far and so thin it will be one long slide into darkness. The other posits that the expansion process will reach its limit at some point and, like an elastic band, will begin to contract at an accelerating rate until it's made up of one black hole compounded with another, contracting to an infinite density, to the size of an atom – the galaxies washed down the drain, and the drain pulled down after them.

At this point the speculation ends, and our crystal ball of physics grows dark. Is that the end? Or, is this another beginning?

Deep questions, from deep space.

In the final reckoning, whichever end theory you choose, Old Father Time will account for everything, and the last rites on an impossibly vivid story will be one last star shining its brilliant dying light on an empty universe, witnessed by no living thing.

And then, dear reader, the universe will arrive at the place where it all began, in a true and total darkness...

ACKNOWLEDGMENTS

A book is much more than the sum of its parts, and although the writing period is quantified in terms of months, the practice of nightwalking has been going on for me for twenty-eight years. To that end, this book owes its debt of gratitude to countless influences from practitioners and enthusiasts who have unwittingly shaped the course of my book. Because you don't know who you are, I name you here with much gratitude and humility.

Stewart Edmondson, Jon Cree, Alan Dyer, Ray Mears, John Rhyder, Rebeh Salisbury, Tom Hills, Martin Shaw, Bill Plotkin, Geneen van Haugen, Steve van Matre, Joseph Cornell, Professor Keith Critchlow, Hugh Lupton, Ashley Ramsden, Roi Gal-Or.

There are also the stalwarts working behind the scenes in Chelsea Green to acknowledge for their patience and perseverance with me making all the predictable mistakes as a first-time author. In particular, credit must go to Susan Pegg for her forensic attention to detail in the copyediting process, and to Fern Bradley for her general forbearance and vision.

LINKS AND RESOURCES

Naturalist Equipment
Watkins & Doncaster: www.watdon.co.uk
Batbox: www.batbox.com

Natural History
Natural History Book Service: www.nhbs.com
The Mammal Society: www.mammal.org.uk
UK Moths: www.ukmoths.org.uk
The Wildlife Trusts: www.wildlifetrusts.org
Bat Conservation Trust: www.bats.org.uk
The Royal Society for the Protection of Birds: www.rspb.org.uk
British Trust for Ornithology: www.bto.org
Buglife: www.buglife.org.uk

Astronomy
Royal Astronomical Society: www.ras.ac.uk
The International Dark-Sky Association: www.darksky.org

Storytelling
Society for Storytelling: www.sfs.org.uk

Campfire Songs
The Virtual Campfire: www.virtualcampfire.co.uk

Wild Events & Training
WildWise Events: www.wildwise.co.uk

Institute for Earth Education
UK: www.eartheducation.org.uk
USA: www.ieetree.org

Sharing Nature Worldwide
www.sharingnature.com

SELECTED BIBLIOGRAPHY

Bang, Preben. *Animal Tracks and Signs*. London: Oxford University Press, 2001.

Boot, Kelvin. *The Nocturnal Naturalist*. Newton Abbot: David & Charles, 1985.

Briggs, Katharine. *A Dictionary of British Folk-tales in the English Language*. London: Routledge, 1991.

Burton, Robert. *Animal Senses*. Newton Abbot: David & Charles, 1970.

Caduto, Michael J. and Joseph Bruchac. *Keepers of the Night*. Golden: Fulcrum, 1994.

Cashford, Jules. *The Moon*. New York: Four Walls Eight Windows, 2002.

Cornell, Joseph. *Sharing Nature*. California: Crystal Clarity Publishers, 2015.

Cree, Jon and Marina Robb. *The Essential Guide to Forest School and Nature Pedagogy*. London: Routledge, 2021.

Dewdney, Christopher. *Acquainted with the Night*. London: Bloomsbury Publishing, 2004.

Ekirch, A. Roger. *At Day's Close*. London: Phoenix, 2005.

Fry, Stephen. *Mythos*. London: Penguin, 2017.

Gersie, Alida. *Earth Tales*. London: Green Print, 1992.

Gooley, Tristan. *Wild Signs and Star Paths*. London: Sceptre, 2018.

Griffiths, Jay. *Kith*. London: Hamish Hamilton Ltd., 2013.

Hislop, Susanna. *Stories in the Stars*. London: Penguin, 2014.

Horowitz, Seth. *The Universal Sense*. New York: Bloomsbury, 2012.

Johnstone, Keith. *Impro for Storytellers*. London: Faber & Faber, 1999.

Knight, Sara. *Forest School for All*. Newbury Park, CA: SAGE Publications Ltd., 2012.

Krupp, E.C. *Beyond the Blue Horizon*. New York: HarperCollins, 1991.

Mears, Ray. *Bushcraft*. London: Hodder and Stoughton, 2002.

Plass, Maya. *RSPB Handbook of the Seashore*. London: A&C Black, 2013.

Plotkin, Bill. *Soulcraft*. Novato, CA: New World Library, 2003.

Raymo, Chet. *The Soul of the Night*. New Jersey: Prentice-Hall, 1985.

Sandberg, Sigri. *An Ode to Darkness*. London: Sphere, 2019.

Shaw, Martin. *Scatterlings*. Devon: Cista Mystica Press, 2016.

Van Matre, Steve. *Sunship Earth*. Indiana: American Camping Association, 1979.

Wills, Dixe. *At Night*. Basingstoke: AA Publishing, 2015.

White, Jonathan. *In Tides*. London: Trinity University Press, 2017.

Yates, Chris. *Nightwalk*. London: HarperCollins, 2012.

INDEX OF ACTIVITIES

INDEX

ABOUT THE AUTHOR

Aubrey Simpson

C hris Salisbury founded WildWise in 1999 after many years working as an education officer for Devon Wildlife Trust, where he worked with Stewart Edmondson, who illustrated the pages in this book. With a background in the theatre, a training in therapy and a career in environmental education, he uses every creative means at his disposal to encourage people to enjoy and value the natural world.

Chris directs the acclaimed Call of the Wild Foundation programme for educators-in-training as well as Where the Wild Things Are, a rewilding adventure based at Embercombe in Devon.

He is also a professional storyteller (aka 'Spindle Wayfarer') and was the co-founder and artistic director for the Westcountry and Oxford Storytelling Festivals.

For further resources relating to this book please visit www.wildnightsout.co.uk.